Why Do People Act That Way?

And What Can I Do About It?

DR. MYKE MERRILL

Published by Fifty20 Communications

ISBN (print): 978-1-893610-18-7
ISBN (e-book): 978-1-893610-19-4

Editor: Rachel Shuster
Cover Design: Deana Riddle, BookStarter
Cover Graphics: Empty Cage Productions
Author Photo: Yeoman Photography

Printed in the United States of America

Dedicated to

my delightful and ingenious wife Pam,

our adventurous and resilient children and their spouses
Matt & Angie, Tim & Kirsten, Katie & Gabe,
Josh & Paula, Mary & Mark,

and our inquisitive and imaginative grandchildren
Malachi & Téa
Ethan, Eli, Micah, Abigail, Claire & Judah (eh?)
Caleb, Seth & Lilah
Jacob & Colton
Jonathan & Holly

from whom I have learned so much and to whom I am devoted
forever.

MBM

FOREWORD

WHY do people act that way? It is not just *a* question, it is *the* question. How many times have you wondered silently or with someone else, why did they respond that way? Inside the pages of Dr. Myke's book you will begin understand the answers to that very real and basic question.

Over the past 30 years, human social skills have continued to wane as people become seemingly more connected, but are really being more isolated via virtual connections on the internet. No, this book is not anti-anything, it is pro-building healthy communication, understanding and relationships.

As a sociologist, professional educator, father, colleague, and friend I've known this author for over 30 years. During my own personal darkest time of my wife's death, he helped me greatly using these tools you will find in this book. I hope you travel with us on this journey unraveling the question: Why do people act that way?

Michael E. Wilson, West Coast consultant and trainer for
Why Do People Act That Way?

CONTENTS

Introduction

Storyline 1*: You are out for an evening walk, and see several neighbors in a tight circle, obviously having a conversation about something. It seems at a glance that it's pretty serious. You walk up and greet them in a friendly manner, but no one says anything back immediately. That's strange. One lady dabs a tear from her eyes. After a few strained seconds, one guy tells you that your neighbor two doors down from your house has committed suicide at his home, today, right around noon. You are stunned. Shocked! You just talked to him last weekend and he seemed "fine." He appeared to you to have everything a modern person could ever dream of having. But he took his own life. The klatch of folks begins speculating on his depression, his problems, his history...None of these speculations adds up at all in your mind. Why do people do that? Not only why do people who seem to have it all together commit suicide, but why does everyone seem to believe it's OK to chatter and gossip about why they think it happened? Seriously, why do people do that?

Storyline 2: You are out to lunch with a couple of friends. While you three are in a secluded booth, one of your friends begins to cry quietly. You ask, "What's wrong?" After an interminable thirty seconds of silence among the three of you, during which you hardly want to breathe, your friend mumbles, "I've been having an affair with someone at work. I think I'm going to lose my marriage." The other friend, stony-faced, with no apparent emotion at all, says, "Aw, don't worry about that. I'm having an affair too. It's no big deal." Then both friends look at you, like you're supposed to say something now. Why do people act that way?

1

Storyline 3: In your work group, one individual is quite skilled, obviously intelligent, has a great work ethic, and very positive productivity. But that person finds ways of "joking" about co-workers, bosses, vendors, customers, passers-by, politicians, family members, and the cleaning staff. Pretty much anybody. But the "jokes" come out in ways that are insulting, crude, mean-spirited, and totally unnecessary. These are always made in under-the-breath comments that are intended only for you to hear and laugh at. The jokes are actually funny occasionally and show intuitive insight. The comments never actually cross the line into reportable violations of company policy. They are never heard by others for verification of your potential reporting. This person seems to undermine relationships with just about everybody, but not openly... So, you know the feigned compliments and encouragements that occasionally come from the offender toward others are part of the great joking mind-set. There's nothing you can say or do about it. Why do people act that way?

You can add to these stories your own "head-scratcher" anecdotes. You simply can't imagine why in the world someone would do something like that. You have no strategies in mind to deal with such situations. You have no idea what to say or do.

It's not just what people do. It's why they do it. The one key aspect in all the mystery seems to swirl around "emotions." That's what seems to be so confusing. Human beings have hundreds of different emotions; they ebb and flow in puzzling ways. It seems impossible to figure out. Not only in others, but in myself.

Many situations may seem benign or insignificant—just people being human beings. Some events are very important. Most of the time, folks just want to get a handle on what's happening, and why people act the way they do.

Over a very long time, as I listened carefully to people of all ages and situations, I developed a theory that there are really only five basic emotions, five systems into which all human emotions can be understood. Our perceptions flow into our emotions. Our motives and behaviors flow out from our emotions. The wheelhouse, which is where the mystery lies, is in our emotions.

> ## There are only five basic emotional systems.

People have problems. That's human.

People get emotional. That can be scary. Or confusing. Or frustrating. People hate being put into a box. That's also human.

From middle school on, I was one of those people many people would turn to in order to talk out their problems. Friends would talk to me. Strangers would unload their situations. I was "a good listener." This phrase means I usually had no idea what to say. I had little or no advice to give. That's quite OK, because I quickly discovered most people don't actually want advice, even if they say they do.

I got a lot of education in psychology and counseling through both my undergraduate and graduate programs. This formal training was based on a clinical model of diagnosis, therapy, and prognosis. I was trained to recognize various mental and emotional conditions, a "box" with set boundaries. I was trained:

- to know how to associate which symptoms lead to which "box," and develop a diagnosis

3

- to treat that "box," so I can recommend one or more options the person can do to deal with that box—therapy

- to estimate how it will probably work out—a prognosis

I learned how to put a person into a box. Most people hate that.

I found very quickly in real life that what I was trained to do in the classroom did not work well in the real world, most of the time. Of the hundreds of people I have worked with, pretty much everyone wants to talk about their perceptions, emotions, motivations, and behaviors. But they don't want "to go for counseling" on everything they feel or think or do. The vast majority of helpful conversations I have had with most people is in what I call "sharing stories." The "sharing stories" can take place in any ordinary human circumstance—a restaurant, a living room, a car or plane ride, a social event—anywhere, anytime. It's a conversation wherever life happens.

A "sharing stories" conversation includes:

- Chatting with a colleague before or after a meeting event, or during a break

- A husband and wife conversing about the events of their day

- Seeing a friend in the grocery store aisle, and catching up with each other

- Four friends playing cards in an evening

- A parent talking to a child about questionable behavior on some topic

"Sharing stories" is not a formal counseling appointment, during which a therapist or trained counselor is interacting with a client in a professional setting. It's what happens outside that kind of controlled situation. It's the normal stuff. A professional therapist might have ten or twelve appointments for sessions in a heavy day. But that same therapist might have fifty or more "sharing stories" conversations in a day, with staff, family, strangers, friends, passers-by, or colleagues. The therapist cannot turn the conversation into a "free" therapy session, regardless of the relationship with the other person.

That's especially dangerous if the other person is the therapist's own spouse.

Real people in the normal course of life don't follow the psychology textbook or laboratory processes. Almost never was I able to consult the standard resources to know what to say or do as a conversation unfolded in real time.

I am providing some foundational concepts and skills that took me decades to develop. You can build on them, reword them, develop them, or discard them. This is the way human knowledge and skill grow best.

Seriously, why do people act that way? And what can I do about it?

Most situations in life are benign. You are neither troubled nor puzzled by them. An event occurs, is resolved (or not), and passes from your attention. Such an event is no big deal. But events do happen that bother you. It might be an observation. You scratch your head and wonder, "Why do people act that way?" It might be a reflection: "Why do I act that way?"

> ## What five emotions do you think there are? Stop a minute and think about it.

When I am engaged in a conversation with someone, I listen carefully to two vital aspects of that person's communications: **what** the person says (the words chosen) and **how** the person says it (the flow.) Of course, nonverbal cues, gestures, facial expressions, body language, tone, pauses, and all the other aspects of communication are important too. But I give special attention as I listen to the words chosen and the expressive flow. Here is an example of what I mean, using the title of this book. A person might say those six words in six different ways, each suggesting a very different meaning. The italicized and bold word in each sentence below is emphasized with a slightly higher pitch and increased volume, as you read each one:

1. *WHY* do people act that way?
2. Why *DO* people act that way?
3. Why do *PEOPLE* act that way?
4. Why do people *ACT* that way?
5. Why do people act **THAT** way?
6. Why do people act that *WAY?*

Each sentence has exactly the same words, but the communication of what that person is frustrated or amazed or confused by is revealed by the flow of the expression, not just the words themselves.

In the following chapters you will be introduced to what I call the four Complexes (Perceptions, Emotions, Motivations, and Behaviors,

6

or PEMB), which independently and interactively form a person's understanding of reality and their place in it. We can begin by considering each Complex as an independent and identifiable aspect of our experience. The first complex includes ten Senses of Perception. Human beings react and respond to perceived aspects through emotional experiences. The bulk of this book is devoted to the Complex of Emotions through a framework of five Basic Emotional Systems. These five systems are named Acceptance, Exposure, Empowerment, Depletion, and Celebration. Emotions stimulate each person's own Complex of Motivations, which includes thoughts, values, habits, viewpoints, and other mental processes. Out of our motivations, the Complex of Behavior includes actions taken as well as actions not taken, both of which are choices.

Once engaged, these four Complexes become interactive, affirming or altering any of the four in many different ways, leading to the frequently thought or spoken question, "Why do people act that way?" (or using similar words.) What seems nearly impossible to imagine will become clear with this book.

Here is the basic flow:

Chapter 1 – The Four Complexes (PEMB): What is Reality?

Chapter 2 – Acceptance: "Love" and its Family

Chapter 3 – Exposure: "Fear" and its Friends

Chapter 4 – Empowerment: "Anger" and its Teammates

Chapter 5 – Depletion: "Sadness" and its Co-Workers

Chapter 6 – Celebration: "Happiness" and its Neighbors

Chapter 7 – The Fifth Complex: The Rule of Capacity

Frequently, after fairly lengthy conversations I have had with people interested in this topic, I am challenged to summarize that entire conversation briefly, in less than ten words. An hour's conversation in ten words? I have come up with this summary:

> # Emotional accuracy leads to effective emotional resolution.

That's seven words. Emotional accuracy leading to effective emotional resolution—that's what this book is all about. I am hoping that you will develop a clear framework to understand better how emotions work generally, and specifically how your own emotions work. That accuracy in description and understanding can provide a basis for emotions to be resolved effectively, rather than be suppressed or repressed, denied, ignored, or left lingering.

This book is published in printed form and electronic for different kinds of readers. It is also presented in an online seminar for those who prefer that method of learning. Live presentations at training events or conferences of any size adds a third means by which these concepts and skills can be gained by those who benefit from interactive, on-site training opportunities.

So, let's get started.

* **NOTE:** Every Storyline described in this book is a composite description from many contributing anecdotes from real people's lives. None describes a specific individual or a particular situation. These Storylines have been carefully written to illustrate concepts and demonstrate principles throughout this book. Care has been taken to avoid assigning gender, age, ethnicity, orientations, religious or political

affiliations, or any other factor which might limit the general human experiences everyone can and does share in, except when it might incidentally make the story read more smoothly or is an essential part of the anecdote.

These three Storylines will be revisited as part of the final chapter.

Chapter 1

What is Reality?
And How Do We Experience It?

Storyline 4: A mother of four children, each approaching adulthood in various stages of late adolescence, walks through her darkened living room around 3 a.m. She smashes her shin into some object left in the middle of the living room's open area, right in the walkway. A sure bruise! Her perception of reality at that moment is that some invisible obstruction, about twenty inches high and having inflexible edges, weighing about forty pounds, was rudely left sitting in her path, probably by her lazy, inconsiderate, seventeen-year-old son.

The mother, incensed, mutters obscenities under her breath, but perceiving everyone is still asleep, she resolves to remain relatively quiet and to really let that son have it when he wakes up in a few hours. Good mom.

Rubbing her throbbing shin, she sits on the couch and turns on the light to examine her blossoming bruise. She glances up and sees the obstruction in the middle of the walkway: a suitcase. A military suitcase. Her oldest son's military suitcase. In about three seconds, her understanding of absolute reality becomes an illuminated understanding of interpreted reality: her oldest is home from boot camp a half day early! He must have driven most of the night to get here! She screams in delight, shrieking that her baby is home! She wakes everyone up! She no longer considers her wounded shin of any importance at all—it doesn't even hurt! She jumps up and races to his bedroom, yelling all the way! Great mom!

Alas, you thought you were getting a resource about emotions and behavior, and now it turns to philosophy! Not really. For you to understand and apply the concepts I will present, we need a common base of definition for the terms I will use. You might have, and probably do have, different definitions for some, many, or all of the terms I will use. I am aware of that fact and celebrate it for the purposes of diversity and independent thinking.

Nonetheless, I am presenting the concepts I hold and use, giving also the definitions of the terms I employ, as a foundation for shared understanding and learning. If your definitions for these terms are the same as mine, our conversations or interactions may be quite easy. If we hold similar but not identical definitions or understandings for the terms we use, our communications may be challenging or even difficult. But if your definitions conflict with mine, they may be merely different, or they might be antagonistic. Our conversation and cooperative learning will be nearly impossible. So, we have to start with the basic terms and their definitions, as I am using them in this resource.

Reality

What is reality? The word "reality" is a noun, giving title to what is described as "real." We use many associated words in English based on "reality":

- Reality – a noun

- Real – an adjective

- Really – an adverb

- Realize – a verb

- Realization – another noun, based on the action of realizing

Conventional wisdom (which we assume must be true) presents "reality" as a fact. What is "real" is not imagined, not made up. It is independent of the observer. Reality "exists," somehow separate from anyone's experience of it.

Seems very scientific and concrete. But that definition is what I call "absolute reality." I use the word "reality" and its associated words in a slightly different fashion, what I call "interpreted reality." I use this following definition for "reality":

Reality is the interpreted perception of what exists independently of the mind interpreting it.

For many centuries, possibly millennia, what is "real" has been the subject of human philosophy, religion, literature, science, and people staring up into space during a dark night and seeing billions of stars and wondering if they themselves really matter at all. Somewhere along the line, children learn how to "lie." They exaggerate, deny, create, shift, change, or adjust "the truth," based on their need for safety, for heroism, for surprise, or just because they want to. Parents and other authority figures demand, "Did that really happen? Is that real?"

What is real? How do we know it's real? How do we describe it, or even think about it? Is our memory of an event real? Is it accurate? Does one's memory line up with a single camera lens or audio recording of an event from a different vantage point? Is some event that triggered a very strong emotion in us real, or only in our minds?

An essential human aspect is the ability to develop a personal interpretation of random events, and infuse that interpretation with meaning, while retaining a sense of one's own self as an identifiable part separate from yet also within that interpretation.

Let's reconsider Storyline 4 again, to consider the concept of interpreted reality.

Storyline 4: *A mother of four children, each approaching adulthood in various stages of late adolescence, walks through her darkened living room around 3 a.m. She smashes her shin into some object left in the middle of the living room's open area, right in the walkway. A sure bruise! Her perception of reality at that moment is that some invisible obstruction, about twenty inches high and having inflexible edges, weighing about forty pounds, was rudely left sitting in her path, probably by her lazy, inconsiderate, seventeen-year-old son.*

In this Storyline, reality is an "invisible object, about twenty inches high and having inflexible edges, weighing about forty pounds." The second part is the dynamic aspect missed by such a stale definition of reality: "rudely left sitting [there] probably by her lazy, inconsiderate, seventeen-year-old son…" That's an internal interpretation of her perceptions, which has become her perception of reality.

The mother, incensed, mutters obscenities under her breath, but perceiving everyone is still asleep, she resolves to remain relatively quiet and to really let that son have it when he wakes up in a few hours. Good mom.

Rubbing her throbbing shin, she sits on the couch and turns on the light to examine her blossoming bruise. She glances up and sees the obstruction in the middle of the walkway: a suitcase. A military suitcase. Her oldest son's military suitcase. In about three seconds, her understanding of absolute reality becomes an illuminated understanding of interpreted reality: her oldest is home from boot camp a half day early! He must have driven most of the night to get here! She screams in delight, shrieking that her baby is home! She wakes everyone up! She no longer considers her wounded shin of any importance at all—it doesn't even hurt! She jumps up and races to his bedroom, yelling all the way! Great mom!

Did the absolute reality change at all? No. Still a forty-pound suitcase with sharp edges left in the walkway of a darkened living room, just about shin-high. But suddenly, the interpreted reality changed radically. It went from a stimulus for grumbling to a stimulus for joy. Same suitcase, different interpretation.

A mass of molecules with specific densities and forms sits in place by gravity, and other molecules in the form of human skin and nerve cells collides briefly with the former molecules, causing an electrical burst traveling along the neural pathways to the brain, stimulating a pain response and startle reaction to draw the skin away from the sharp edge...absolute reality. No interpretation. No meaning. Just an event.

But reality as experienced by human beings has to be an interpretation of the molecules and events involving those molecules. In the dark, a banged shin and muttered curses forms one interpretation of the molecular collision, but in the light, an emerging child-adult home safely is an entirely opposite interpretation of the exact same events. Which one is "real"?

So, let me repeat my definition of Reality:

Reality is the interpreted perception of what exists independently of the mind interpreting it.

Human beings exist in a realm involving a location on a habitable world within a solar system within a galaxy within an intergalactic system within the universe. Human beings are extremely complex living organisms with the ability to interpret their surrounding objects and events with meaning, significance, values, and understanding. Human beings do not live in an absolute reality. We live in an interpreted reality. We use our senses of perception to gain input about the environment surrounding us, and our minds to interpret those perceived objects and events.

Why is this whole discussion on reality important in understanding why people act the way they do? When I am trying to figure someone out, and, much more, trying to figure myself out so that I can be helpful in working toward resolutions of complicated relationships and events, I start at a conceptual foundation of reality. I do not ask, "What is absolutely real here?" I ask, "How do I (or this other person) perceive the reality of the situation? What is real to me about this? What is real to the other person, in their interpreted perception?" I cannot just guess, or estimate, or make up what I think. I want to inquire, investigate, and listen. I want to understand where we're starting from.

I have a reasonable working definition of reality so far. That's where I am starting this discovery process. What's next?

Four Complexes

The human experience of reality occurs in four Complexes, which begin in a predictable and observable sequence, but the four complexes become interactive and interdependent once engaged. A "complex," as I am using the term, is a set of abilities, partly biological and partly learned, by which each person receives and interacts with reality as each one interprets it. Simple titles for these four complexes are

- Perceptions

- Emotions

- Motivations

- Behaviors

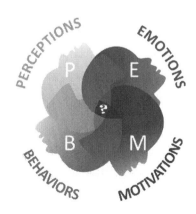

Let's consider each of the four complexes in turn, and then look at how they function sequentially and interactively.

Complex 1: The Ten Senses of Perception

You probably learned in elementary school that human beings have five senses of perception: sight, hearing, taste, smell, and touch. We use our eyes, ears, tongue, nose, and skin as the means by which stimulations from the world may be perceived by the brain. While true in basic terms, this limited list is quite incomplete and overly simplified  to the point of being misleading. I hold that human beings have ten senses of perception, all functioning with many variables of acuity and capacity, by which each person's brain gains, stores, and accesses information, allowing for interpretation in many ways, resulting in an awareness of "Reality."

Whenever I am in a conversation with someone, I try to keep an awareness that he or she expresses thoughts based on the total variables of *their* perceptions, not mine, adjusted slightly or significantly based on values and intentions that person has. That is, the person might have seen, smelled, or sensed something in a particular way, and have a variety of feelings about it. He or she might communicate a true view of their thoughts or be lying outright. All those variables are true for me too.

It's a wonder that human beings can communicate with each other at all.

These are the ten senses of perception:

1. The Sense of Sight

Obviously, human beings can see, or at least most of them can. The eyes are the organs that can most sensibly perceive "visible light," which is, in reality, a very tiny sliver of all electromagnetic energy. Most people can see shapes, black and white. and their various shades, a few million colors in the "ROY-Gee-BIV" schematic (red, orange, yellow, green, blue, indigo, violet.)

All the variables that might exist in any particular person's vision will affect *what* that person sees through their eyes; interpretation and un-derstanding manage *how* the person perceives and thinks about what they have seen.

One more very important point: you actually do not see with your eyes. You see with your brain. What I mean is this: your eyes pick up a very slender sliver of all the available radiational energy being generated or reflected from a source. That light energy is "processed" on a "visual platform" in the brain, which the mind engages and interprets.

For example, here is a word I want you to look at:

Look carefully. It's a word. It's not a picture of two eyes on one side of a face, with a unibrow on its side and an open mouth below the eyes. Is it clear in your vision? Look away. Can you rewrite that word accurately? Do you understand what you saw? Will you remember it next week? In two minutes?

Your eyes see it clearly. Your brain's visual platform presents it clearly. But you do not derive any meaning from what you see, unless you can read Korean. Then, of course, you see "ppang." Of course, that's obvious now, isn't it? Sorry, you don't understand "ppang"? It's the Korean word for "bread." Your eyes could "see" the word, but your mind could not understand what you see, so you cannot understand it, read it, remember it, or repeat it. Where was the failure?

It could be in your ocular system, with a disease or distress somewhere in the many parts of the eye or nervous system. It could be in the visual platform of your brain. It might be in your lack of education or loss of attention or forgetfulness. But you see with your brain, not your eyes.

2. The Sense of Hearing

Most human beings can hear, within a certain limited range of tone and loudness. The ears are the primary organ for hearing sounds which come through vibrations in the air. Some sounds, such as the deep bass of gigantic woofers mounted in the back end of a car passing you, can vibrate your chest cavity, and some hypersonic squeals can pierce your head and give you a splitting headache. Again, only a small range of all available sounds can be heard by human ears.

3. The Sense of Smell

The olfactory system of human beings is found primarily in the nose, but also interacts and depends on the gustatory system of the mouth. Both the sense of smell and taste function through chemoreceptors. Smell works as a distance chemoreceptor and taste works as a direct chemoreceptor.

4. The Sense of Taste

The gustatory system of human beings is found in the tongue and mouth, allowing people to sense the flavors of sweet, salt, bitter, sour, and umami (savoriness.) Some cultures add piquancy, or the "hotness" quality of certain pepper oils, as a distinct taste.

5. The Sense of Touch

The largest organ of the human system is the skin. Amazingly flexible and complicated, sensors in the skin perceive pressure, temperature, pain, and texture. Sensations of touch can at times be ignored, such as the weight of your clothing or wristwatch, while even the slightest variations in any factor may initiate immediate and intense awareness, such as an insect alighting on your neck or a speck of sand working its way into your shoe.

6. The Sense of Balance

The vestibular sensory system is found in the inner ear and controls the sense of balance. The vestibular system constantly monitors the body in relation to the world around it, as to its balance point. Losing or gaining weight changes one's balance and can make a person feel constantly "out of sorts." Getting up quickly or making a sudden motion can affect the sense of balance, and consequently one's composure or comfort level.

7. The Sense of Position

The proprioceptive sense is perceived by the skeletal system. As surely as the ears hear sounds or the skin feels heat, the bones sense physical position in space. The proprioceptive sensors are the bones, joints, muscles, and sinews of the human body.

The sense of position in space allows people to perceive where they are in the context of the world around them, where the "world" is and the limits of their own bodies. A person with a poorly functioning sense of position may not even know why he or she feels "out of sorts" frequently and be at a loss about what he or she cannot perceive. This might sound very odd to you, but very young children, rapidly growing teenagers, and elderly adults may sometimes knock over their drink glass, spilling the contents, because their skeletal systems are changing, and they cannot tell exactly where their hand is at the end of their arm in space relative to the glass. Their eyes can see fine, but they don't reach out and grab hold purely by hand-eye coordination. The proprioceptive system is in play. It's hand-skeletal coordination.

8. The Sense of Memory

The ability of the brain to remember stimuli from the past can provide contemporary impressions that might be as "real" to a person as any present item. The range of energy that memories might have stretches from mild to overwhelming.

An ever-present challenge is that one's memories may be unrelated to anything in the environment shared with you. A person with whom you are speaking may be remembering a wide range of benign and potent memories, stimulated by any factor in the total environment (or by nothing apparent at all.) You may or may not even be aware of the memories of the other person, and how those memories impact the conversation.

9. The Sense of Imagination

The creative sense can provide stimulation that is neither from the current environment nor recalled from the past. The sense of imagination can be well-developed in one person, even specifically to certain kinds of creativity, while in others this sense is virtually nonexistent.

10. The Sense of Psyche

The psychic sense may include spiritual phenomenon, an awareness of non-material realities, or other stimuli from dimensions that cannot be examined scientifically. The human soul is the means by which the psychic and spiritual realm may be perceived. This area, of course, cannot be examined or measured by currently available equipment, but that alone does not disprove its existence. The sense of psyche might also include perceptions that cannot be explained by any other means.

Complex 2: The Five Basic Emotional Systems

Key to conversations and relationships with others is understanding emotion. The Complex of Emotional Systems is what this book is primarily concerned with. I have developed a framework of grouping several hundred various emotions into five dynamic systems, each containing forty-five or more concepts in an ascending column of increasing  intensity. Each system of emotion has a primary goal, or agenda, which all the associated emotions in that system drive toward accomplishing or resolving. The five emotional systems are not listed in any particular order of importance, or likelihood of expression, or value.

No commonly held definition exists for what an emotion is. In my study of the writings of dozens of psychologists, psychiatrists, counselors, and neuroscientists, I found no commonly held definition of "emotion," even by two of them. It seems none of the experts can precisely define what "emotion" is. One attempt at an explanation comes from Dictionary.com: "*1. an affective state of consciousness in which joy, sorrow, fear, hate, or the like, is experienced, as distinguished from cognitive and volitional states of consciousness. 2. any of the feelings of joy, sorrow, fear, hate, love, etc.*" That's pretty vague.

The Merriam-Webster online dictionary gives a broad second definition for emotion in three parts:

a: the affective aspect of consciousness: FEELING

b: a state of feeling

c: a conscious mental reaction (such as anger or fear) subjectively experienced as strong feeling usually directed toward a specific object and typically accompanied by physiological and behavioral changes in the body

Strong feeling? Not always. Typically accompanied by physiological and behavioral changes in the body? Too limiting for the full expanse of emotions humans experience. I was positioned to develop my own working definition of "emotion." I define an emotion in this way:

> # An emotion is an affective reaction or response, based on a person's perceptions of reality, providing a link to motivations and behaviors.

Emotions may be mild, moderate, or intense. A person experiencing emotion may have a word to title or describe any certain feeling, but perhaps the person is too young or too old or too distracted to apply any word accurately. An ability to verbalize accurately how an emotion can be titled is not an essential aspect of an emotion. Emotions are the initial link between perceptions and motivations.

I gave a title to each of the five systems that was completely neutral. Emotions are not "good" or "bad" in themselves. All these titles are words used for other contexts with other meanings. One emotional title might appeal more to you as a representative of that whole system, rather than the words I chose. I am content for everyone to develop their own ways of defining and engaging these concepts. These are my titles, selected after significant grappling with language that will be broadly understood and easily utilized.

In this preview of the Five Basic Emotional Systems I will present three aspects for each system:

- the main title and brief description of each emotional system,

- a brief description of the primary objective of each system, and

- several sample concepts in ascending order of intensity within that system group.

I termed a group of associated emotions to each main title with a word that suggests ways in which people work together: a family, friends, teammates, co-workers, and neighbors. These five ideas are equal and random—it's how I understand emotions to relate to others within each system. The emotions are not competitive or oppositional to each other, but cooperative and connected. In each of the five systems, the group of emotions is described as "neutral." The concept of neutrality expresses that each of the emotions is neither automatically "good" or "bad," a positive emotion or a negative emotion. Each emotion simply exists; it's what you do with them that bends them.

In each of the next five chapters of this resource I will present a more complete view of these systems. This section is a brief overview, to present the four complexes and how they engage and interact, as a foundation for the concepts I am presenting.

1. The Emotional System of Acceptance:

"Love" and Its Family

Acceptance is the emotional drive for a person to attract, possess, consume, or retain a person or an object. Feelings of Acceptance at any intensity level motivate a person to bring closer what is away. The "neutral family" of Acceptance emotions may consist of curiosity, liking, preference, love, devotion, craving, addiction, and obsession, along with other "siblings."

2. The Emotional System of Exposure:

"Fear" and Its Friends

Exposure is the emotional drive for a person to seek safety or security from danger or risk. Feelings of Exposure motivate a person to protect, hide, cover up, or avoid a threat. The "neutral friends" of Exposure emotions may consist of shyness, embarrassment, nervousness, fear, guilt, shame, and terror, along with many other "friends."

3. The Emotional System of Empowerment:

"Anger" and Its Teammates

The emotions of the Empowerment system drive a person to control, dominate, or effect change in a person or situation. The system inspires a person to accumulate power, and to win. The "neutral teammates" within the "Empowerment" system may consist of bothered, annoyance, frustration, anger, competition, fury, and rage, plus additional "teammates."

4. The Emotional System of Depletion:

"Sadness" and Its Co-Workers

Emotions of Depletion lead a person to restore resources, rest, or heal. Sometimes it is supposed that Depletion, or its common depiction, depression, is either a negative emotion or the absence of emotion. Instead, Depletion is a positive, valuable emotional system, which incites a person's drive toward recovery, replenishment, and restoration. The "neutral co-workers" in the area of Depletion may consist of hunger, tiredness, sadness, grief, woundedness, exhaustion, being overwhelmed, and more beyond these "co-workers" listed here.

5. The Emotional System of Celebration:

"Happiness" and Its Neighbors

Feelings of Celebration work to motivate a person to shine, share, expand, or give of themselves outwardly. The "neutral neighbors" of Celebration may consist of contentment, happiness, joy, gratitude, generosity, thrill, and compulsion, plus other "neighbors" too.

A quick summary of the five basic emotional systems:

- "Love" – **Acceptance**: To Attract or Possess

- "Fear" – **Exposure**: Gain Safety or Security

- "Anger" – **Empowerment**: Get Power or Change

- "Sadness" – **Depletion**: Gain Rest or Recovery

- "Happiness" – **Celebration**: To Shine or Share

Complex 3: Motivations

Though this Complex is simply titled "Motivations," it contains countless aspects of the processes human beings use to connect emotions to behaviors. Motivations include, but are not limited to,

- drives

- habits

- thoughts

- values

- traditions

- practices

- intuitions

- viewpoints

- attitudes

- prejudices

- experiences

- plans

Newborn babies have fewer innate drives, but everyone is born with some genetically-based motivations. "Startle" at being suddenly dropped, "pleasure" at being cuddled, "sucking" to be nourished, "focus" at a human face eight to twelve inches away, "distress" at cold or wetness or pain, are all built into nearly every human being. On the rare occasion that one or more of these genetically-based motivations are diminished or not present, the likelihood of survival is severely compromised, if not impossible.

As human beings grow and mature, new phases launched by bodily changes, hormones, and experiences can initiate a completely new interior environment by which a person discerns reality. Emotions change radically, which affects how perceptions are developed and experienced about reality. In turn, these changes alter the connections to motivations in all their varied aspects. Correspondingly, as aging, disease, environmental factors, experience, and other factors change for a person, all of these aspects are affected as well.

How do emotions engage motivations? A very few responses are autonomic—self-generating without any thought process required. For most people, a very sudden sharp sound causes a startle reflex instantly. One might think about the sound and its source and meaning after the jump, but that instant twitch does not require values or history or thought. But for the vast majority of human experiences, perceptions trigger emotional engagement, which then stimulates the motivational complex. Each person's motivational complex is unique. No two persons have exactly the same sets of thoughts, values, habits, or impulses. For example, I was a volunteer firefighter for a couple years. One Halloween night, some kids set a giant mountain of tires on fire, using gasoline as an inflammatory igniter. The firehouse siren went off, and I raced to the facility along with quite a number of other volunteers. I was very new at this service, while most of the other men in that company had years of experience. We raced to the site of the fire, and before the truck was fully stopped, one guy about my age raced off the platform straight for the worst area of the giant blaze. I was cautious, thinking through my training, calculating the danger of further explosions, wondering if my jacket and helmet would protect me adequately from the fire and the heat. I was moving toward the fire, but very cautiously, due to my lack of experience, my mental juggling of issues, and my imagined risk of being burned alive by an avalanche of burning tires.

This other young man sprinted toward the fire, and in what I thought was a display of utter stupidity, ran almost into the burning pile. He was just to the left of the hottest part. He started heaving tires from one section back toward me and yelled for me to get them and roll them away from the area, down a slight grade. As we worked like maniacs, sweating more than I thought I had moisture in my entire body, a team of about five men carved a valley through the tire pile, separating the lower, burning section from the much higher mountain that hadn't ignited. This young guy knew the tire pile, how they were

28

interlocked, that they were stable and wouldn't cascade in an avalanche, and that burning rubber is nowhere near as hot as other combustibles. His emotions were drive, determination, engagement, and passion. All that adrenaline-fueled emotion connected with his history, knowledge, training, and awareness. He was confident and effective. I was scared and hesitant.

Complex 4: Behaviors

Behaviors are the fourth Complex in the sequence of experience by which human beings exist in reality. The fourth Complex is as varied and vital as the third one is. Each person develops literally millions of behaviors. Some of these behaviors are so habitual as to be subconsciously performed or avoided, and some of which may be conscious and regular. Some behaviors may be unique, done only once in a lifetime.

Behaviors fall into two branches: engaged and disengaged. I am not using those terms as moral valuations, meaning good or bad. An engaged behavior is an action taken. It is something done outwardly. A disengaged behavior is an action not taken. It is something avoided.

Here is an example of an engaged behavior versus a disengaged behavior, both of which are a decision to act in a certain way. Your neighbor is walking his dog near your home. Actually, it's technically not his dog; it's his wife's dog that he is walking. You see the dog hunch up and you know it is going to make a deposit on your lawn. This neighbor does not carry pick-up bags. Ever.

You see the dog and the neighbor. You feel welling up a nasty annoyance about the impending pile and the total inconsideration that it expresses. You are just about to blurt out a mean-spirited insult, and you remember the neighbor's wife passed away three weeks ago. Technically, you now suppose, it is his dog now.

You have lots of perceptions, including smell, sight, and memory. You have lots of emotions: disgust, anger, weariness. You have many thoughts simultaneously, including awareness of the man's loss, the little trouble it really is to clean up the mess for him, and your rights to a clean yard. So…do you say something (an engaged behavior) or do you not say anything (a disengaged behavior)? You have a choice of either action: speak or be silent. Both are options you "do," even though one is outwardly active and the other is outwardly passive.

How the Human Experience Becomes Interactive

All human experience begins with the complex of perceptions, when the person has one or many of the senses stimulated. These perceptions excite the complex of emotions, triggering mild, moderate, or passionate feelings. The emotions then engage the complex of motivations, drawing on a huge number of thoughts and strategies. Finally, the motivations elicit the complex of behaviors, and the result is engaged or disengaged actions.

The four complexes can be described in a linear sequence, which is how they start: perceptions, then emotions, then motivations, then behaviors. The four complexes have launched. But from that point, the sequential structure of the four complexes ends, and the four complexes become interactive. They are in dynamic flux at their intersections. These intersections affect the experience; any of the complexes can be altered by any of the complexes, including itself.

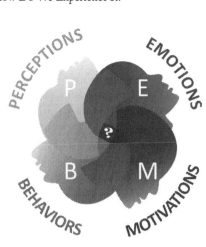

Let me illustrate this concept. You are sitting in your office, sipping coffee. Without warning, a very loud, sharp "BANG" occurs just outside your office door. What actually happens in that moment and the next few seconds?

Something produced a loud, sharp sound. The sound traveled through the air to your ears in about $2/100^{th}$ of a second. Your ears received the loud sound and processed it, in about one quarter-second. Your very first response was the startle reflex, through the amygdala of your brain, near the brainstem. Your body jumped a little, involuntarily, spilling your coffee slightly. You had a number of autonomic reflexes, such as the hair on your neck rising, your muscles tensing, your adrenal glands secreting a bit of adrenaline, and your pupils dilating slightly so you can see better. You might have blinked. All these responses might have taken one-half to three-quarters of a second. You still have not thought consciously about the meaning of the loud sound.

After your instantaneous startle reflex, you begin to think about what you heard, and what it means. You instantly consider several possibilities. Was that a gunshot? Perhaps some idiot threw a firecracker. Maybe someone just slammed a book shut or slapped a ruler on a desk. You heard the sharp report clearly, but at this moment, you cannot remember exactly what it sounded like. You then evaluate each possibility in light of both your experience and your knowledge

31

of recent events. If you seriously consider the possibility that the sound you heard was a gunshot, you might respond in one of several ways. You could immediately run to the door of your office, open it with appropriate caution, and investigate the situation, because you are trained in emergency situations and are personally prepared to act courageously. Or, you could immediately run to the door of your office, slam it shut and lock it, push a chair under the handle, and hide under your desk, because you are frightened terribly by the possibility. Though you yourself might never consider running *toward* a gunshot sound, that might be an appropriate response for some people who have different experience and makeup than you.

If you are accustomed to the sharp sound of a sudden loud bang near your office door, you might not have any startle reflex at all. If you are very easily alarmed by such a loud sound, you might not be able to stop shaking and have to take the rest of the day off, even after you find out someone just slapped a ruler on a desktop. You will have one or more emotional responses in conjunction with your thinking process. All of these responses might take one to five seconds. You take certain actions (engaged) and avoid other actions (disengaged.)

From this moment, everything becomes interactive. Your senses are on high alert, so your eyes and ears are much more attentive to every sound and sight. Your heart is pumping more rapidly, and you are thinking very quickly. Every detail is being stored in your memory, so as you recall the experience later, you might feel like everything was happening in "slow motion." Your fear, or courage, as the case may be, now affects your thoughts dynamically. Your thoughts interact with your perceptions, which also affect your emotions, and even your actions become interactive with all the other aspects of your experience.

Had the loud sound never happened, you would have sipped your coffee, finished your task, and completely forgotten about the day after a week or so. Since the loud sound happened, you will never forget this moment as long as you live.

This example shows in an anecdote how human beings experience the world and their place in it. Perceptions, emotions, motivations, behaviors...and all of them dynamically interactive with the others as an event occurs.

Now, the Five Basic Emotional Systems, one at a time. These systems are presented in random order, not by importance, feeling, or experience.

Chapter 2

The Emotional System of Acceptance and Its Family

The first emotional system is Acceptance. This system may include the emotions of affection, preference, love, craving, and obsession. It is resolved when the object of desire is obtained in some way. Consider some situations to illustrate this system.

Storyline 5: You have a fourteen-year-old son, a normal boy who never cleans up his room, hates taking showers, eats everything in sight, is sullen, grumpy, or miserable, based on the day (or maybe even the hour.) He has grown seven inches taller in the past eighteen months, ruining several pairs of shoes and wearing pants that would be appropriate for wading in four-inch deep water. Suddenly, one morning, he passes through the kitchen on his way to school, his hair washed and combed, and you catch the scent of aftershave cologne wafting off him. Why would he act that way?

Ah, you know. He has a girlfriend. His first crush. He's in love. What do you say as he heads out the door?

Storyline 6: You are at a celebration picnic event. Every kind of delicious grilled and baked food is laid out on long tables, and the serving line winds along slowly on both sides of the tables, plates loading up to the spill level as your co-celebrants prepare to gorge themselves. You spot your absolute favorite picnic item at the far end of the table: perfectly grilled Italian sausage smothered in onions and peppers, or baked garlic Brussel sprouts and asparagus tips, or a scrumptious California sushi roll with one piece left. Your mouth is watering. Just as you approach that part of the table, a wide spot on your plate all prepared for your absolute favorite food, the guy right ahead of you on the other side of the table, with his plate already piled high, grabs the last piece OF YOUR FAVORITE FOOD! The last piece! Why would somebody do that?

He's a *Sus scrofa domesticus*. (That's a pig, species name.) That much is obvious. But what do you do next?

Storyline 7: Another mass shooting makes the news, this time in your state. You work in a "soft target" environment, like a school or nightclub or church or market. This time, you know and all your co-workers know it could have been your place. You have a workplace dialogue session about prevention and procedures, but eventually the conversation focuses on Second Amendment rights and why people want guns. One person in your group, for whom you have significant respect for their intelligence and productivity, is rigidly insistent that absolutely no compromise on gun ownership is possible, regardless of how crazy or criminal people use guns or how much modern firepower they have or how many victims are hurt, killed, or suffer life-altering losses in their families and communities. No. Compromise. At. All. Why does a smart person hold such a ridiculous, dangerous position?

And what do you do when working with this person? You have to, but how?

These three Storylines all deal with varying intensities of Acceptance emotions, from fairly mild to moderate to intensely passionate. In the three anecdotes presented, you and the other participants in the scenes are dealing with different expressions and intensities of this system.

The System of Acceptance is a scale of emotional responses linking interpreted perceptions to drives of obtaining, having, possessing, consuming—drawing the object of desire from away to closer.

Looking at the graphic of The Emotional System of Acceptance below, you can see eight emotional titles, moving from left to right and up the incline, which identify different intensities within the emotional system of Acceptance. A person's emotional state will be very different based on the object of the feelings of Acceptance and can increase or decrease over time based on many personal factors for the individual.

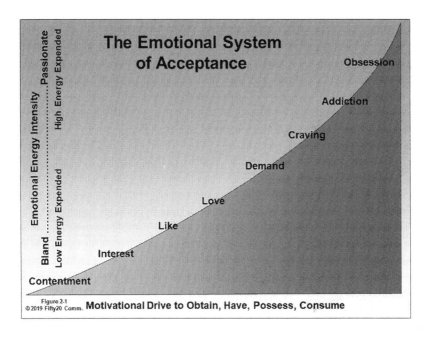

Figure 2-1
© 2019 Fifty20 Comm. **Motivational Drive to Obtain, Have, Possess, Consume**

Keep in mind that the words I use within this system are not absolutely defined or scientifically stacked. After listening to people of all ages and cultures, I organized into this structure those emotions and feelings which I heard repeatedly. It is not fixed, nor exclusive of your observations and thoughts. It reflects a general pattern of how feelings of Acceptance escalate or wane, based on many variables and factors. The main key is to observe and understand, rather than control and predict.

Reconsider the three Storylines as examples within this system, focusing primarily on the system of Acceptance emotions.

37

Storyline 5: Your fourteen-year-old son is "falling in love." No use of "love" from earlier in his life has prepared him for feelings of attraction and relationship he is now experiencing for the first time. Since Day One, you have been affirming your love for your son. He is loved, cherished, desired, connected, bonded. In his entire lifetime of fourteen-plus years, just past five thousand days so far, he has heard about love and been the object of love hundreds, if not thousands, of times. Here is a brief summary of his "love life" so far:

- Parental love = Mommy and Daddy love you

- Love for parents = Mother's Day cards say, "I Love You, Mom!"

- Family love = Don't torture your sister like that! We love each other in this family!

- Pet love = I love my dog

- Sports love = I love playing baseball/football/hockey/video games

- Food love = I love broccoli and cheese sauce

- Prominence love = I love the spotlight

- Friend love = Luv ya, Bud!

- Fast food love = McDonald's: I'm Lovin' It!

- Music love = "Love you, Babe!"

- Championship love = Our team won because we love each other!

- Beatles love = "All you need is love!"

But now, there is something so completely new about a relationship with another person that there is not only an exclusion of all other people and his relationships with them, there is an exclusion of all other definitions for "love." He has never felt anything like this new passion. It's a different drive altogether.

He is practicing what "love" is and learning both internal and external boundaries for love. He is learning to make new definitions for words that he himself has used and have been spoken or written to him. He is working to understand new facets of one-on-one relationships, and commitments that lead to and flow from these feelings. This new "love" thing is very complicated for someone with just five thousand days' experience.

Those feelings may be reciprocated by the object of his affection (the girlfriend), but they might not be. That is not particularly relevant at the moment. He has moved up the scale of Acceptance emotions with regards to this young female, and that changes everything. He is growing up, and the changes in his body and culture inspire him to see himself and others differently, smell himself and others differently, touch himself and others differently. He might not use these words, but his feelings can verge on infatuation, or possibly obsession, or maybe even addiction toward this girl. Two weeks ago, he talked incessantly about his "loves" of sports, games, buddies, adventures. The toy car collection now draws no interest from him at all.

So, what do you say as he is walking out the door, scenting the air with *Intimately Beckham* (a popular aftershave cologne), not daring to look you in the eye or hesitate even briefly lest you say something really bad? You have about one second, and this specific moment is gone forever. You can make this about yourself and make some comment which might embarrass him or challenge him. That kind of comment will elicit a response of Exposure or Empowerment (dealt with in upcoming chapters.)

Or, you could make a comment that matches his feelings of Acceptance. "Looking good today, Bud!"

Be ready for the rejection, the crash, the failure of first love. It will likely happen, sooner rather than later. His love and affection will drop, possibly right out of sight for a while. You can support him and admire the process. You can anticipate he may become obsessive or craving or even pretend to be disinterested or merely interested. You cannot learn this system for him. He has to discover it and practice it.

Storyline 6: In your own scale of Acceptance emotions, you have gone way past interest, liking, preferring, or loving your favorite food. You crave it! Except having and enjoying it, no other option comes close. Your sight, smell, and taste buds were all activated by your increased desire, and you fixed your expectations based on the assumption of its availability and its proximity to your possession. Then, suddenly, an individual whose passion for that very same food was obviously much less than yours, and whose personal need for it was far below yours, had the advantage of position to step in and grab the food you wanted...needed...craved.

So why would he do that? He was hungry, and it looked good. He considered his appetites and tastes, and that particular food matched his preferences. He was in a long food line with lots of options, and lots of people in line, but did not expend any effort or thought in whether someone behind him might want or crave the food he was taking the last of. He's not actually a pig, just kind of oblivious, but hungry.

You, however, are left with an Acceptance quandary. That food is what you zeroed in on having, and you increased your drive to have it, consume it, own it. You can achieve that objective by speaking up just as you first see him reaching for what you are craving. That not being possible, since he already took it, you can substitute another option on the table that will satisfy you just as much, or nearly as much. Or you can abandon the idea of having it now and build a plan to fix your own portion within a day or so.

Using words to describe with absolute precision a feeling or a thought you have is close to impossible. Not only is the language itself not sharp enough to divide every nuance of an emotion into all possible sections, but interpersonal and internal boundaries interfere with such precision.

For some reason, at the precise moment of make-it-or-break-it, the guy who swiped the last piece of your favorite food glances back and catches your eye. In a split second, he reads in your eyes the desire for that delectable delight, now perched on the top of his own mountain of food. With a small hint of surprise, he says to you, "Oh, did you want that?" He gestures toward the prize which is still causing your mouth to water. What do you say now, at this exact moment?

"No, that's OK. I'll get something else."

"Um, I really did want that. I mean, I really, really, really wanted it." (Add more "reallys" if you want to intensify your communication.)

"I wanted that particular piece enough to kill for it! That's my absolute favorite food in the entire world, maybe the entire universe!"

"You already touched it. I can't eat it now. Thanks a lot."

"On a scale of 1 to 100 for desire, I'm at about a 650 for that food. Give it to me!"

You might not know what your own exact feeling is, nor what you are willing to do to get that food. That concept is not only true for you, it's also true for every other human being. Everyone struggles to communicate what they perceive, feel, think, and do exactly. It's tough being human.

Storyline 7: We now get beyond the fairly benign issues of daily life and enter an aspect of modern life that is of the utmost importance. In many discussions, respect for another person's opinions, lifestyle, rights to privacy and possessions, and viewpoints is generally assumed and granted on all sides of the conversation. To each his own.

But there are some topics that bring about instant passions, and the emotions are intense and often unyielding at any level. People can hold to their viewpoints rigidly, and the stakes can be very high. In terms of Acceptance emotions, when a person is faced with holding onto his or her passionate ownership of a specific position *or* having the respect and camaraderie of co-workers, family members, friends, neighbors, or strangers, maintaining the rigid position might win out over the relationships with others. Can we agree to disagree? Sometimes, the answer to that question is, "No. Period."

You might think that result is illogical and unreasonable, and you would be right. You might think such a stance is absurd and ridiculous, foolish. Obscene. Impossible. And you would be right, according to your own scale of Acceptance emotions, what you perceive through all your resources and then connected to what you are motivated to do. But as we said before, the sequence of perception-emotion-motivation-behavior happens at the initiation of an experience. After that start-up, all four complexes become interactive, and change each other in very dynamic ways.

Your co-worker holds what you consider to be an indefensible position, taking into account the lives damaged and lost by gun violence in the modern age. But some set of factors and forces has driven your colleague's emotions upwards on the scale of Acceptance, now pushed up to an addiction to that position, or an obsession with the concept of private gun ownership. How can that happen?

The use of the word "addiction" in this concept is not equal to physical or psychological addiction to drugs, alcohol, or any other addictive substance or activity. I am using the word "addiction" as an emotional word, which may or may not be as simple as a conscious choice or intensified desire.

You and your colleague both have a personal worldview, how you understand reality to function with you in it. Remember, absolute reality is impossible; interpreted reality is how human beings actually function. When you offer a proposal that pits the value of a single human life against the collective right of millions of individuals to own a mechanical device (gun) that has the potential to launch a projectile explosively in a particular direction, you might think you're just being sensible. According to your worldview, the answer is clearly evident. One human life is worth more than the collective rights of millions of people. However, with that logic, we also need to get rid of cars, planes, bicycles, alcohol, knives, and on and on. You have tapped into an area of your colleague's life that is not merely a preference or a desire. It is way above that.

Your gun-loving colleague may actually have a softened view that entertains some reasonable restrictions on gun ownership. However, he has a perception that the workplace environment is slanted "to the left," and most of the co-workers are tending toward a liberal position on many topics. His defense of the Second Amendment, and the specific interpretation of the wording there to mean private ownership of any weapon, is hardened by his held value that "if you give an inch, they'll take a mile." His action, defending a particular interpretation of the Second Amendment, is adjusted by his perceptions, emotions, and motivations as experienced in that moment of discussion, as well as generally in this time period of his life. His action, and your reaction, affect the emotions he feels about the issue.

You are faced with an Acceptance issue. In your personal makeup as a person, can you continue some kind of connection with a person whose values, thought processes, worldview, and political positions are in friction or conflict with your own? Do you have the personal capacity to associate with that person or not? Both are valid results, if you can assess the situation accurately and appropriately. Make a good decision for yourself and act on it to bring about a result you can manage.

How Can "Love" Ever Be a Problem?

A conventional view of emotions pits "positive" emotions against "negative" emotions. Some emotions are imagined as always good, while others are always bad. There is something essential in the emotion itself that makes it a good one or a bad one. I don't hold that view at all. All emotion is neutral with regard to its moral or ethical value. No emotion automatically is a good emotion, and no emotion is essentially a bad emotion.

The concept of love is a good starting place to grapple with this concept. Love, in the system of Acceptance, is a moderately-to-significantly intense drive to attract, draw near, possess, have, hold, or own. But it's just a word, which ultimately can mean whatever its user intends. It can be modified by adding adjectives, adverbs, and all manner of expressions to communicate how intense the love is.

- I love you

- I really love you

- I really, *really* love you (and so on…)

- I am so in love with you

- I fell in love with you

- I'm head-over-heels in love with you

- I love you so much it hurts

You can continue this list for quite a number of additional entries. A person may express love for a food, a person, or an activity. The point is, love can verge on a craving, an addiction, or even an obsession, which can reduce a loved person down to an object to be held and owned, in the mind of the lover. A young child often "loves" a particular toy, blanket, or other item so fiercely that the child will not share it, will not let go of it, will not allow it any freedom at all. Parents then teach a child to "love less," or scale down the drive to an affection or a preference.

Teens and adults can also intensify love until it is unhealthy. A person feeling and expressing love at a certain intensity will not consider allowing the beloved person, object, or opportunity any escape. No one else can approach or befriend the beloved. The drive becomes exclusive, perhaps both to the lover and the beloved and all others in any relationship to either one. This extreme level of love is not producing good and is not beneficial in any way. An obsession, in the emotional system of Acceptance, comes into play when the person narrows the field of focus from all friends to just many associates to only a few contacts down to a single object of desire.

It also is possible to have too little drive in the system of Acceptance. As a child emerges into adulthood through adolescence, he or she may reduce the affection previously held for many objects and relationships from childhood, slowly or suddenly. The child-becoming-adult no longer loves the toy cars or dolls or activities or friends that shortly before had consumed the majority of attention and time. But now, "Oh, I don't care!" is the response to presenting the formerly loved item.

Adults who have had relationships of bonding and connection can fall out of love, and either drift or become antagonistic, even brutal, toward the one previously beloved.

Though an observer may want to manage and control someone else's likes and loves, the practical role one can have is to observe and interpret.

Resolving Emotions of Acceptance

Emotion is the affective link between perceptions and motivations, resulting in behaviors. But all the complexes become interactive, once engaged. The emotions in the system of Acceptance are resolved, or realized, when the person is able to obtain, have, possess, or connect with the object or person of the desire. Desire can, however, be unsatisfied, incomplete, by not being able to resolve. Three outcomes are possible:

1. **Achieve** – obtaining or drawing the object of desire is completed

2. **Alter** – the object of desire cannot be obtained, but an acceptable substitute is obtainable and resolves the desire

3. **Abandon** – the object of desire cannot be obtained, and the desire comes to an end and is no longer desired

If none of these three resolutions completes the emotional system, the energy devoted to it may grow more intense, and the feeling moves up the scale. The person will make more effort toward resolving the emotion with achieving, unless altering or abandoning occurs at the higher level.

Storyline 8: A young adult male, age twenty-two, has every legal right to own whatever type vehicle he wants and can afford. When this young man was a boy of ten, he got his first ride on a small minibike. That first ride was absolutely thrilling to his young mind. He was smitten with the need for speed. He wanted a full-sized dirt bike, but his parents did not believe he was physically or psychologically mature enough to operate one properly. He was not permitted to get one.

Did that end his desire for a fast motorcycle? Hardly. He covered his walls with posters of motorcycles. He watched motorcycle races of all kinds. He built model motorcycles. He took rides on friends' bikes whenever he could, without telling his parents. He got video games of motorcycle races. His desire intensified and was unresolved.

He loved motorcycles. He craved a motorcycle. Nothing else would satisfy his growing addiction for speed and thrill on a powerful bike. After twelve years of intensifying drive to have a powerful motorcycle, he bought his very first one: a 1200-cc "crotch rocket" that could go zero-to-75 in about 4.5 seconds. You finish this story:

1. He got six tickets for speeding in two months, lost his license for a year, and gave up the bike for a more sensible street ride.

2. He lost control on a curve at about 120 MPH and died tragically.

3. He joined a riding club with other need-for-speed guys and had a blast riding safely on the roads and racing on a local track built for motorcycle racing.

4. He ran that bike for two years, sold it, and bought a 1700-cc superbike.

5. He found out riding fast wasn't all that thrilling, compared to other pursuits and relationships in his young adult life, so he

parked it in the garage and there it sits.

6. He won the national title for motorcycle racing, got tons of endorsements and won lots of money, and retired at age twenty-nine.

7. He drives around town like a ten-year-old in a twenty-two-year-old's body, burning rubber and having neighbors shake their heads at the comic scene.

8. Add your own ending.

A more complete view of the Emotional System of Acceptance is shown on the next page. The mild emotions are at the bottom, the moderate emotions are in the middle, and the intense emotions are at the top, with an arrow pointing up as intensity increases.

Emotions do not flow in nice, neat, straight sequences, properly moving up or down this kind of scale in order. You might not include some of these words as aspects of Acceptance at all, while you might find that people with whom you are in a relationship or just in their vicinity may use other words, expressions, sounds, body language, or gestures. The exact words are not the important aspect of this concept. It is that emotions fit together in a system, with similar factors and driving toward similar outcomes.

At a mild level, this emotional system is more easily satisfied or resolved when the object is achieved, altered, or abandoned. Not much energy, including time, effort, finance, or focus, is expended in accomplishing the drive of obtaining or having or possessing. At a moderate level, more energy will be put into the obtaining or possessing of the object. At a passionate level, excessive energy will be expended to draw the desired object in, including a complete unwillingness to give up the pursuit.

OBSESSION
Craving
Addiction
Demand
Adoration
Intimacy
Cherishing
Breathless
Embracing
Delight

LOVE
Bonding
Security
Devotion
Romance
Expectation
Fascination
Camaraderie
Anticipation
Intention

TRUST
Affection
Preference
Friendship
Care
Attention
Desire
Infatuation
Enjoyment
Neighborliness

LIKE
Attraction
Fondness
Inquisitiveness
Curiosity
Sympathy
Interest
Tolerance
Want-Need

SATISFACTION

What Can I Do About It? Set the Preferred Outcome!

This question seems simple at the first read, but it has a hidden complexity. What am I able to do about it? More than that, what am I willing to do about it? What do I want to do about it, but can't bring myself to do? What do I want someone to do about it, but I am not going to be a part of that action? A skill in any situation is to determine what is your preferred outcome, and the challenges that exist for you.

Reconsider Storyline 5 in a much broader, family context. What is the ultimate outcome of raising children? What are the boundaries that permit or restrict what you can do? In the permitted boundaries, what aspects are required or essential and what aspects are allowed or discretionary? Describing your objective in clear language helps greatly in knowing what boundaries apply to the question at hand.

In this Storyline, you have a fourteen-year-old boy experiencing his first romantic love. At any particular moment, you yourself (as the parent) might experience confusion, amazement, frustration, or happiness over the antics of a mid-adolescent trying to navigate through these uncharted waters, as far as his experience is concerned.

Let me propose four options for the ultimate purpose of parenting:

1. To raise obedient children

2. To fulfill my own dreams or continue my legacy through my children

3. To do unto others (my children) what was done unto me

4. To raise successful adults through their childhood in my home

Consider carefully each one of those statements. Does that particular statement lead to certain boundaries for your choices? Does each one rule out certain choices and actions that cannot be engaged because they would thwart or interfere with that ultimate purpose?

If the parent of the fourteen-year-old boy considers each of these goals in turn, how might that one moment occur?

1. "Stop right there, boy! I want to see what you're wearing and what you're up to!"

2. "Hey, Slick! Don't do what I wouldn't do!"

3. "You stink! You think any girl is going to be interested in a punky kid who smells like that? Give it up! She'll dump you in a second. She's not worth it! Hey, come back here! I'm talking to you!"

4. "Looking good today, Bud!"

What might be the imagined responses of that fourteen-year-old boy, within the goal as stated by the parent, but not necessarily accepted by the child himself?

1. *Zoom, out the door with no response at all. The parent is left yelling at the door. The primary options are rebellion or a broken spirit of submission.*

2. "Whatever that means!" *The primary options are resistance or compliance to an agenda that child did not choose.*

3. "Yeah, shows what you know! I'm not you!" *The primary options are aggression or loss of personal identity.*

4. "Thanks!" *The primary options are success or failure, both of which contribute to maturity.*

Choosing the best possible objective sets the best possible boundaries, and thus the best possible actions in any given situation.

A child growing up is not a piece of property to be owned or a pet to be trained. A child growing up does not exist to replicate or continue the parent's life or legacy. A child growing up does not earn love through performance.

A child growing up is preparing for the majority of his or her adult life. When this is your preferred outcome, you can choose your response to this young man much better.

Chapter 3

The Emotional System of Exposure and Its Friends

The second emotional system is Exposure. This system may include the emotions of shyness, hesitation, fear, shame, and terror. It can resolve when the object of insecurity is avoided, or safety is gained in some way. Consider some storylines to illustrate this system.

Storyline 9: You and three colleagues are at a small restaurant for a lunch meeting of a work group, which has been assigned a task within a great project. Your collaboration is important, and you have ordered a light lunch in order to devote as much time and energy to productivity as possible. The colleague to your right suddenly shrieks very loudly, pushes back from the table violently, knocking the chair over and pulling the tablecloth nearly off the table. Drinks are spilled, plates are askew, and silverware flies. Everyone at your table and nearby tables are wide-eyed with surprise.

You look over at your colleague, who is shaking perceptibly, face drained of color, eyes wide, focused on the tabletop, hands covering the mouth. "What?" you manage to say after about two seconds, having no idea what just happened. "That!" your respected colleague gasps, pointing at the messed table. "Oh," says the friend across the table from you. "A *Parasteatoda tepidariorum*. (Poignant pause, for dramatic effect.) A common house spider." That super-brave soul takes a butter knife, deftly slides it under the spider, creates kind of a cup with a napkin to contain it, and gently carries it to the nearest doorway and tosses it outside. Why do people act like that around a harmless spider?

Storyline 10: You are a teacher who has a class of twenty-two children in second grade, all around seven or eight years old. You notice after a number of weeks that one child plays actively with the others on cloudy days but refuses to leave the shaded area by the building on sunny days. Absolute refusal. No amount of encouragement or gentle pressure works. One sunny day, you sit down beside the child in the shade and ask, "Can you tell me why you won't play with the other kids today? Everyone wants you to come play." The child says, "I hate my shadow." Why would a child say that? More importantly, why would a child hate their own shadow, enough to refuse to play in the sunshine?

Storyline 11: You have lived in a quiet neighborhood next-door to a wonderful young family. In this neighborhood, everyone watches out for each other, carefully being aware and observant of what's happening. You saw something this morning that has you concerned. Flashback twelve years: your neighbor has a child that is two years old, and occasionally runs out in the front yard totally naked. It seemed cute at the time, the parents chasing their toddler this way and that way to at least get a diaper put on their precious offspring. Your mind zooms through memories from the past twelve years to the present moment. The child peeing in the front yard once, at age four, completely naked. This same child walking the dog at age seven, completely naked (the child, not the dog.) It clearly is not a frequent thing. You have just a few memories of spotting this child completely naked out in public, and even those memories are brief moments. It was cute, then puzzling.

Then, this morning, the child walked out in the front yard to retrieve something, completely naked, now about fourteen. Obviously maturing now, this mid-adolescent seems to have absolutely no embarrassment over public nudity. None. Do you say something? Is it against the law somehow? Shouldn't a person have any decency at all about their bodies available for public viewing? In today's world, even in the safest neighborhoods where people watch out for each other, isn't it dangerous for anyone to have no protection for their bodies in public, regardless of what they do in their own homes? Why would a child of that age do that?

The System of Exposure is a scale of emotional responses linking interpreted perceptions to drives of protecting, hiding, or covering— gaining safety and security.

Looking at the graphic of The Emotional System of Exposure below, you can see eight emotional titles, moving from left to right and up the incline, which identify different intensities within this system.

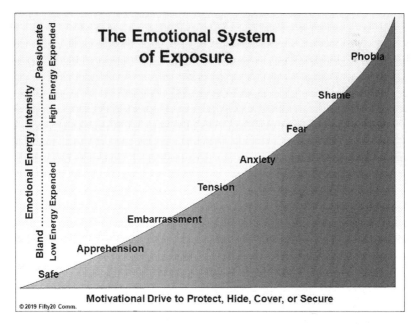

You might use different words or stack them in a different way. Everyone has individualized ways of feeling and expressing these emotions; prescribing ways in which someone should or must display emotions of Exposure will be neither helpful nor necessary. Any of the emotions in this system, stimulated by interpreted perceptions and leading to motivations and behaviors, share in common a drive for safety and security from some kind of threat or danger. That sense of danger may be mild or extremely intense, and may come from something seen, heard, smelled, remembered, or imagined. The perceptual source is irrelevant to the feelings.

Let's review the three Storylines presented above, focusing particularly on the emotions of Exposure in each one.

Storyline 9: Your respected and very capable colleague seated to your right has a phobia about spiders. You all at the table can laugh about it, try to ignore it, share your own discomforts or phobias, or try to talk your friend into a more logical and reasonable reaction to common house spiders, compared to tarantulas or black widows. However, those approaches probably will not help your respected colleague. The reaction to the sight of a spider, instantaneous and extreme, is not a reasoned or a reasonable response.

Your friend experiences a passionate level of Exposure, a complete and absolute loss of safety and security the moment a small eight-legged creature is perceived. But why? Any number of early childhood experiences might provide insight to that person or to other supportive friends, which may shed light.

1. At the age of three, in an event that cannot be consciously recalled, your associate was suddenly awakened by a spider that had let itself down into the crib and was crawling on his or her eyelid. The startle response was extremely intense, not knowing what was happening, or how to do anything about it. The sight, combined with the tactile sensation in a person who has heightened sensitivity in both those senses of perception, was enough by itself to generate a lifelong phobic reaction to any image or actual presence of a spider.

2. Your colleague, whose mother also has severe arachnophobia, recalls at age nine that his father, uncle, and older brother

thought it would be hilarious to tease him with using their hands as crawling spiders all over his body, hair, skin, and even in the air nearby. The teasing actually became torment, and the mockery and shame forced on this now-adult person as a very emotional preteen sealed the system of Exposure as a necessary response to any repeat of the stimulus. A spider in any form generates embarrassment, fear, shame, and terror, all up and down the scale.

3. Your friend, while camping as a late adolescent, was bitten by a spider. The bite caused a moderate allergic reaction that included nausea, redness, itching, and dizziness, though some of those biological reactions might have been caused by poison ivy at the same camping event. Nonetheless, being a person with great sensitivity to the vestibular sense and being unable to stop scratching at an irritation until it bleeds and becomes infected, he totally associated all the discomfort solely on the spider bite. For your friend, a rapid avoidance response is logical, appropriate, and, in fact, necessary.

Storyline 10: A child who will play outside on cloudy days but not on sunny days? Fear of sunburn? Is the solution to apply SPF 50 sunscreen lotion? That's not it. The child actually gave you a clue as to what the issue might be.

"I hate my shadow."

Hate is a strong word and may or may not be the correct feeling as expressed by an eight-year-old child. You can try some kind of deflective response which disregards the child's potent feelings, such as, "Oh, come on. You can't hate your own shadow. Your shadow is your friend for life!" Rather than patronize or redirect this child, you can explore what is the source of the hatred or to what exactly is it attached.

With some gentle and supportive questioning, over a period of some time, you observe carefully how this child interacts with his or her own shadow. When a cloudy day clears a bit and the sun peeks out, forming a shadow for everyone, you notice something important. The moment the child spots his or her own shadow on the ground, the second grader runs for shade, under a tree or by a wall. And, you notice, when this same child walks by a large window or anything that reflects an image, the child immediately turns away and will not interact or even look at his or her own reflection, even dimly.

Putting lots of pieces together, you may speculate this child is in a family system that uses body shaming as a means of control. It has been driven into this child's mind that a perfect body is of utmost importance, and any imperfections or weight gain or ungainliness is horrible, a significant cause for guilt and shame. You can gently try out your theory: "Do you hate your shadow because you hate your body? Because your body makes your shadow?" If this is actually what is going on in this seven- or eight-year-old's mind, you won't be dealing with hatred, but with shame. The child needs safety and security concerning body image issues. Good place to start.

Storyline 11: This situation presents a difficult social and personal issue. Do you feel embarrassment for the naked teen? Do you imagine yourself caught outside with no clothing on, as if in a nightmare? Is the family next-door a naturalist family, enjoying complete nudity within the household and at restricted nudist camps without any body shaming at all? Are you verging on imposing your own standards of modesty on someone whose personal standards are different? Or, has this child somehow failed to develop an ordinary and expected protection in an open public place, possibly inciting a predator in the vicinity to see an opening?

This is an open-ended Storyline. No simplistic answers or absolutes are possible. The emotional system of Exposure engages based on some biologically ingrained factors, but much more on values, attitudes, and preferences that are expressed in a wide variety of behaviors. Your own perceptions and emotions are interwoven with your values and behaviors, and then they have become interactive in you. So your projected embarrassment may be inappropriate, but your caution regarding potential predatory adults may be legitimate. Both are emotions within the system of Exposure.

Can terror be a good emotion?

Emotions in the Exposure system can be thought of as "bad" emotions. Who wants to be afraid? Feelings of shame or terror, especially when the emotion is intense and unresolved, do not feel comfortable or pleasant. That alone does not make them bad emotions.

Intense emotions are appropriate in certain kinds of situations and circumstances. In fact, if a person does not sense terror (or however one might title highly intense Exposure emotions) when that person is in actual mortal danger, something is wrong. The person's perceptions of the situation have not alerted the potential victim of great harm or tragedy, or the motivations and values needed to secure safety weren't triggered.

An instantaneous startle reaction up to an ongoing terrified state can produce an amazing array of biological and mental defenses. Experiencing emotions of Exposure across the spectrum causes the eyes to widen and the pupils to dilate, allowing a greater awareness of movement in the surroundings. The adrenal glands spurt adrenaline and muscles strengthen. Reflexes quicken. The mind can assess circumstances more quickly, and decisions can be made almost instantaneously. Emotions of Exposure can be extremely helpful in very dangerous situations.

Resolving Emotions of Exposure

In conventional thinking, feelings of Exposure (embarrassment, fear, shame, or terror) produce one of only two responses: fight or flight. However, a third option is also quite viable. The new list of potential responses is:

1. **Fight** – one significant response to great fear is to fight back. One might use a loud voice or expanded motions to frighten back the threat. A person might physically fight back with body actions or weapons of some kind to force the threat away or to defeat the threat, securing safety.

2. **Flight** – another significant response to danger is to run, to flee the situation which includes the threat or danger. A person might hide or move, anything from a flinch to an outright run.

3. **Fright** – a third real option is fright, to stop entirely, to freeze in position. Sometimes referred to as "a deer in the headlights" response, a person caught in a terrifying circumstance can actually shut down, become completely motionless.

The central objective in resolving emotions of Exposure is to attain safety or security. This is a necessary human need, and can be stimulated by an incidental threat, like a single person intending or capable of causing harm, or a universal common threat, like winter coming at the end of the planting, growing, and harvesting cycle. It can be a real threat, such as a predatory relative causing physical and emotional abuse to a child. Or it can be an imagined threat which has no basis in fact, such as an asteroid or meteor streaking out of the sky and hitting a person squarely. It does not matter how a person has perceived the danger and responded with feelings of Exposure. Reality is formed from interpreted perceptions, and so, within the frightened or terrified person, the threat is as real as anything can be. The key question is how to resolve the feelings.

Two realms of safety and security are attainable. One is external and the other is internal. External safety can be a change of the circumstances, either by an alteration of present surroundings or leaving the circumstances for a new location. Internal safety can be a strengthening of personal awareness and capabilities. Either, or both, can contribute to a resolution of the feelings of Exposure.

Storyline 12: A four-year-old child in your family system is under your supervision and care for the night. About 11:30 p.m., the child begins screaming in great fear, crying out for Mom or Dad. You rush into the child's sleeping area and turn on a light. "What's wrong?" seems to be a logical question in the situation. "There's a monster under my bed!" the child shrieks, still trembling visibly and crying hysterically. You sense by smell, sight, and texture that the child has wet the bed significantly. What do you say and do to help this frightened little person? Here are some options:

1. You say, with some impatience, "Stop being a baby and just go to sleep. There's no monsters under your bed." You shut the light off and close the door. *This option ignores the entire source of the fear, and likely decreases the safety the child senses.*

2. You exclaim, "You wet the bed! Now we have to change all the sheets and your pajamas. Maybe you should just sleep in the wetness, and that will teach you a lesson." You pull the sheets off, and the wet clothing, and go through a dramatic changing of all the bedclothes. "I'll leave the door open and a hall light on. Now just go back to sleep." *This choice adds a level of guilt and shame onto the child, and essentially increases the level of Exposure emotions being felt.*

3. You go over and hold the child, regardless of the wet conditions. You say, "There's no monster under the bed. I checked. You're safe now." You calm the child, get a big towel to lay underneath the child for some dryness, and wait for the child to go back to sleep. *This approach brings an external sense of safety in you being present. It might work for a little bit, but the child may awaken repeatedly and need you to come back in the room.*

4. You sit with the child and enable them to calm down, using appropriate words and hugs. Then, you look around the room you're in and spot some small object that the child can hold onto and would cause no personal injury if the child fell asleep with it. "Oh, you are one very lucky child! Here is a Monster Zapper! (It's actually a toy drumstick.) The child retorts, "No it's not! It's just a toy!" "Ah," you say, "only when you hold it this way. But if you turn it upside down, it zaps monsters. They just disappear. Here, let me show you first." So, the two of you get down and pull stuff out from under the bed, holding the Monster Zapper and zapping away any monsters. Then, you give the Monster Zapper to the child and have the previously-frightened little person zap some monsters from the other side of the bed or the closet. Or down the hallway or outside the window. You change the sheets together, checking for more monsters to zap while doing so. You equip the child to internalize the strength to make a safe environment.

This more complex choice validates the fear as perceived by the child and shifts the locus of control from an external source to an internal source.

You might think I randomly included the detail about wetting the bed, but that's not a miscellaneous thought. Human urine has a very strong scent and is an offensive deterrent to many animal predators in the natural realm. No child knows this fact, but it may be an instinctive response to fear that a person urinates. Oddly, it may help reduce a child's fear to get up and go to the bathroom (if the child hasn't done so involuntarily) because of this association. Keep in mind the "monster" under the bed may actually be the wet bed itself, which is under the child, of course. The child is embarrassed and guilty and ashamed and nervous about wetting the bed. These feelings are all friends of fear. If you can strengthen the child's sense of safety and personal ability to manage the moment, you will help the child resolve his or her fears. That security will resolve all the associated emotions within that system.

A more complete view of the Emotional System of Exposure is shown on the next page. The mild emotions are at the bottom, the moderate emotions are in the middle, and the intense emotions are at the top, with an arrow pointing up as intensity increases.

Almost all emotional words have other uses in the breadth of human experience. For example, feeling vulnerable and actually being vulnerable are associated but not identical uses of the word. Feeling naked as an emotional aspect of Exposure is a link among perceptions and motivations and behaviors to hide, cover, protect, or find safety. But being naked is a physical aspect that may have absolutely no emotional attachment at all, just a fact of being unclothed.

Condemnation can be a judicial act, but it can also be an emotional state of experience. Anyone can use any of these words at a mild level, a moderate level, or an intense level. No rulebook sets the standard of how a person may use these words to identify or express feelings. Regardless of the word choice, **discovering** the accurate level of Exposure and being able to **declare** it provide a basis for **determining** the best ways to achieve real safety and security, as well as the perceptions of safety and security.

PHOBIA
Panic-Paranoia
Horror
Terror
Condemnation
Shame
Humiliation
Cowardice
Dread
Reverence-Awe

FEAR
Startle
Nakedness
Loneliness
Powerlessness
Guilt
Fright-Scare
Chill
Breathtaking-Amazement
Stress

ANXIETY
Worry
Tension
Nervousness
Regret
Risk-Suspicion
Weakness
Indebtedness-Obligation
Vulnerability
Inhibition

EMBARRASSMENT
Troubled-Bothered
Timidity
Apprehension
Sensitivity
Shyness
Hesitancy
Caution–Uneasiness
Startle

SAFE

Three helpful ideas in emotional resolution:

1. Discovery

2. Declaration

3. Determination

What can I do about it? Emotional Neutrality

Above all, stop thinking of fear and all its friends as "bad emotions." Fear, guilt, embarrassment, shame, and terror are wonderful emotions in the right place and for the right reason. Exposure emotions are neutral—neither good nor bad automatically. People want to avoid what is bad, so they may have a very hard time embracing their fears or even facing them. It is impossible to resolve an emotion a person refuses to take ownership of. What a person does with their emotions creates the good or the bad.

Emotional Neutrality is a principle of thinking, which guides your perceptions, motives, and actions. Love and Joy are not automatically "good" emotions, and Fear, Anger, and Hurt are not the bad ones we don't want. In the right place and time, for the right reasons, all emotions are appropriate and beneficial. In the wrong time, or the wrong way, or for the wrong reasons, any emotion can be destructive or inappropriate.

Chapter 4

The Emotional System of Empowerment and Its Teammates

The third emotional system is Empowerment. This system provided the greatest challenge to title with a word that was not slanted positively or negatively in the minds of most people. The system of Empowerment can include the emotions of boredom, irritation, anger, competitiveness, and rage. It is resolved when there is a shift in power, or a change has been accomplished. This system is focused on power, winning, and control. Consider some situations to illustrate this system.

Storyline 13: You are part of a sports team, and your team is now in the semifinal playoff round. A lot of prestige and bragging rights are on the line, but no money, unfortunately. One of your teammates is now up, ready to make a big contribution toward team victory. This particular teammate has not performed in peak form in this game, and no one is more concerned and focused than he or she is right now.

You study your teammate's face, as everything in the game is falling into position. You see a face filled with fury, almost rage. It's alarming to you that your teammate could be so angry about a game! You resolve to talk about this at a later time. Why do generally nice people get so angry over a game?

Storyline 14: A customer walks into your store with a computer product he had purchased a couple days earlier. Tagging along is the customer's fifteen-year-old son. You greet the customer by name when they walk in the door, but he does not reply. You had not met the son previously. In a gruff display of annoyance, the customer puts the computer on the counter, clearly upset, and announces in a loud voice that the computer you had sold him was a piece of junk, and you had better make it right or he's calling his lawyer.

Wow! That's quite a leap from ignoring a greeting to a threat of legal action, in about two seconds. The father is front-and-center, arms crossed over his chest, a frown on his face, and daring you to say anything. You have the sense he will jump all over anything you say. Anything at all.

The son is standing to the side of the father, not making eye contact with you nor his father. A thousand issues are racing through your mind simultaneously, but it's your turn to say...*something*. Why do people you are really trying to serve and help do this kind of stuff to you? Is it worth staying in retail business, when you encounter customers like this?

Storyline 15: You are in charge of a small group of kids for a national organization. Generally, these kids are responsible and engaged in the mission of the organization. You conduct all kinds of special activities and events for your group, some occurring for an hour or two and some involving overnight camping or lock-ins. The main problem, which happens just about every time you hold an event of any kind, comes at "cleanup" time.

They're suddenly bored. They're tired. They are finished with the last activity. So, you lay out the plan to clean up, with plenty of warning in advance. They stall. They avoid helping. You get frustrated. You give a warning about not putting on this event again if they don't start the cleanup process right now. They pick up a couple small things, and then turn that activity into a game, which makes a bigger mess. You increase the heat. They don't comply. In a strong voice, you give them an ultimatum. They ignore you. You plead, then command. They start and then drift off out of the cleanup zone to play a bit. You've had it.

You give "the look" that is supposed to wither the most resistant child, but they smirk and mimic your glare with feigned mockery, as only children can do and get away with.

That's it! You're furious, and you let them know it. You're done with this group. Every single time! You've had it! The straw that broke the camel's back has now been added to the pile! You are going to quit leading this group of immature children who do not deserve what you're doing for them. You launch into doing the cleanup by yourself, clearly at the end of your rope on this. And they start profusely cleaning up like maniacs, apologizing repeatedly, grabbing things you picked up and stowing them where they belong. They clean like professionals.

Why do they do that to you? Why can't they just clean up when they're first asked? You're actually not going to quit leading the group. But why does this keep happening?

This system, called Empowerment, is third in random order, not because it is a central core or what a person feels as a middle emotion. The three Storylines above all deal with varying intensities of Empowerment emotions, from fairly mild to moderate to intensely passionate.

The System of Empowerment is a scale of emotional responses linking interpreted perceptions to drives of effecting change, shifting power, attaining control, or winning.

Looking at the graphic of The Emotional System of Empowerment below, you can see eight emotional titles, moving from left to right and up the incline, which identify different intensities within this system. A person's emotional state may be very different based on the persons and circumstances which engage feelings of Empowerment, affected greatly by many variables.

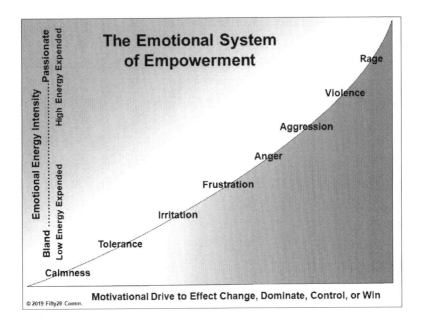

As is true to some degree in all the emotional systems, a person feeling some level of Empowerment may use words or gestures that might make it appear they are lower on the scale than they actually feel, or even higher on the scale than they actually feel. Adjusting the word choice (lower or higher) may be for social reasons, strategic reasons, or just because that person doesn't have a lot of options in his or her emotional vocabulary in this particular area.

Let's take another look at the three Storylines presented above.

Storyline 13: Certainly, highly competitive people can also be easygoing and loving folks. However, the emotion of competitiveness belongs in the system of Empowerment because, at its core, competitiveness is about winning, gaining dominance, control and power. Verbs used for winning a sports contest have a consistently violent or power-focused meaning:

- The home team *beat* the visitors

- The challenger *defeated* the veteran player

- They *snatched* defeat from the jaws of victory

- The defending champions were *crushed* by the overwhelming offense of the new champions

- We *killed* those guys tonight!

You can add many other words of battle, power, or violence to these descriptions of one person or team winning the game. (That sounds *so* boring!) Anyone speaking about a sports game never says, "Our team scored more points than the other team, so we were determined the winners of this competition." Blah!

If you study a person's face when they believe the moment is *now* that winning or losing is on the line, and that winning has a very high value, you will notice the scowl, the knit brow, the focused eyes, the clenching jaw muscles, the hand grip all are identical to a very angry person's face. Competitive people at the critical point of the play do not put on a happy face, do not seem serene, look scared, or seem sad. In a few seconds, they might display any of those emotions, but that's after they made the hit for victory or struck out in defeat.

Your friend is not "angry," *per se,* but is focused and competitive. Being a good player with lots of success in previous games, and in this game having underperformed in a way that hurt the team's chances of advancement, your teammate is linking interpreted perceptions of himself or herself, the team, the score, and the moment's importance to motivations and behaviors that will succeed right now. The facial expression reveals the intensity that person is feeling. If the effort is a failure, that person may display significant anger, verging on rage. If the moment turns out well, instant joy!

Competition and rage are close neighbors in this emotional system and jumping from one to the other can be a small step. Competitiveness can quickly transform into violence and destruction, especially when driven to great intensity by a championship or rivalry. This phenomenon can be seen in a single individual or an entire community.

Storyline 14: The angry customer is very common in the business world. Many people start the process with the belief that they're somehow getting ripped off by retail stores, and that's pinpointed on the salesperson or staff person the customer deals with. The customer comes into the sales situation "loaded for bear," as they say. (That's a hunting expression: instead of being prepared for small game, the hunter is ready for the big game.)

So, as the staff person encountering this already-boiling customer, you have quite a few choices, only three of which I will describe:

1. You meet fire with fire. No matter how nasty and unreasonable this customer gets, you can top it. You match his body position, drawing up to your fullest height, crossing your arms too, scowling, and use a gravelly voice to push back. If it escalates from there, you can always call a manager, or 911.

2. You give up and give in. Whatever the customer wants, the customer gets. The customer is always right. Refund the money and get it over with. The guy gets his money, loudly announces how awful this store is, and storms out, kid in tow.

3. You perceive this entire situation is about power, winning a competition against you, the shop staff person. But, you also sense that this situation is not just about the computer and whatever the problem is with it. The man brought his fifteen-year-old son to "tag along." The son is standing to the side, not

making eye contact with you or with his dad. Why is the son here? What's going on?

You decide it would be best to help the father resolve his anger appropriately rather than boil over or win without a contest. You either sit down if you have a stool or chair or lean over a bit so your eye level is slightly below the father's eye level. He perceives that he has a little bit more power, but you're the one who set that up, so you actually have more power. You're two steps ahead of him now. That's quite an advantage. You ask, very calmly, "Can you describe the problem with this computer? Let's see if we can figure it out." You are joining with him, on his team, to resolve the problem. He might not believe that, yet.

You converse about the problem, as he describes it, and you keep an eye on the son. He's tracking with you, and you guess the son knows more about electronic systems than the father does, and probably could have set the computer up to work properly if the dad had let him. But you will not defeat the father through the son. This is about something else.

You allow the father to make a good point, on anything, which you acknowledge. You notice the father looks at his son with a kind of triumphant smirk, which you'd really prefer to slap off his face. (Don't do it.) But now you know what's happening. This dad brought his son to show him how to do it, how to get your way, how to win in a business deal. The son is not particularly interested in that idea, but he came anyway. You will help the father solve his anger over this issue if you can have him come out looking good to his son. It's not about the computer.

Storyline 15: You have now played the game with these kids, again. They know the rules and you followed them perfectly. You're the one getting played.

1. The event is drawing to a close, and they know the last step before heading home: Clean up! You issue the first call. They avoid, using plan 1. They know exactly what you'll do next.

2. You escalate up the system of Empowerment, but slightly. Your tone, your words, and your actions are now more forceful. They avoid, using plan 2.

3. You escalate again. They avoid, using plan 3.

4. Rinse and repeat. (You escalate again, up the scale. They avoid, using plan 4, then 5, then 6.)

5. Finally, you hit a note, a tone, an action that they know is your breaking point. Actually, not your breaking point. It's your action point. It's the moment in the game when you will actually do something. They know it and start cleaning like professionals.

Why couldn't they just clean like professionals at the beginning of the whole process? That's the game, and kids love to play it. They have learned not to do whatever they don't want to do (clean up, end the event, and go home) until you actually hit the action point. When you are willing to act, they know it. The key: move your action point down to step 2 above. Start your real action when you're annoyed instead of when you're furious. The outcome will be exactly the same, and you won't have wasted a huge amount of time and energy.

Is Anger a Bad Emotion?

Often, anger is treated as an isolated emotion which slides up and down its own scale, from "a little bit angry" up to "super angry." Thus, we end up with targeting anger as a solitary emotional state which needs management; ergo, anger management programs. If anger, however, is understood a teammate of a greater system, and the best outcome is resolution, not management, we can approach and experience anger very differently.

No emotion is automatically good or bad. Anger fits in this concept: anger is not a bad emotion. Anger does have to do with power, dominance, winning and control. So, when a child experiences anger, adults in the situation may not have any idea how to yield power appropriately or teach the child how to win well. If the adult has issues with any level of anger, either experiencing it or expressing it, the solution may seem obvious: *stop* the anger. That actually won't work, because anger is an appropriate human response, given a set of perceptions that link to motivations and behaviors.

Being angry, and even very angry to the point of furious or enraged, can be very helpful in the face of abuse, injustice, or threat. Oddly, when a project is becoming due and a person has procrastinated or been overwhelmed in trying to get it done, a potent spurt of determination or aggressiveness enables quick thinking, greater strength and alertness, and drives focus much better. You might feel exasperated or mad that time is running out, but that feeling can bring about a good result, or mess up the outcome terribly. It's what a person does with their anger that is good or bad, not the anger itself.

Resolving Emotions of Empowerment

Emotion is the connecting link between the complexes of perceptions and motivations, resulting in behaviors. But, as is consistently true, all the complexes become interactive, once engaged. The emotions in the system of Empowerment are resolved, or realized, when the person is able to accomplish a change, win a competition, shift power, or dominate. That resolution does not mean the Empowerment emotion disappears, because factors may continue to exist that stimulate ongoing or even increased Empowerment feelings.

Storyline 16: A single parent has one child with some special needs for services. You are the director of the agency to which the parent has now come, to receive child care services under a contractual arrangement. You inquire of the parent if your county's disability services will be providing some or all of the cost for services. Oddly, the parent bristles at that question, and replies that it is inappropriate for you to ask about their financial status or what disability support they might or might not be receiving or have received in the past. This is odd, because no parent ever has bristled at that question from you before this situation. It doesn't appear to be a big deal, anyway.

You are aware that the child has received services from several other organizations in the area, but one after another refused to accommodate this family to continue providing services. You ask the parent why the child is not receiving services anymore from another service provider. The parent becomes defensive, and asks you why are you being so negative? The parent states that previous services are a matter of privacy, and that privacy is protected, so don't ask. This pushback from the parent seems to be some form of hiding or perhaps aggression. You also recognize that the claim to privacy is absolute. You have no point in contacting the previous agencies to inquire into this family's journey through service agencies.

The parent has registered the child with your organization, paid the registration fee and several months' service costs. Then, payments stop for services rendered. The parent continues dropping the child off at your organization for services, but the parent slips in and out quickly to sign the child in and out, never actually allowing a conversation or confrontation with staff or management.

After several months of nonpayment, the task of dealing with this situation has become your priority. The child clearly needs service support, and your center has the capability and desire to provide it. The parent simply is not paying the weekly fees. You press for a payment, or the child must disenroll from the center. The check is deposited and bounces for insufficient funds. You know this parent actually has the financial means to pay for these services.

You are beginning to suspect why the other organizations refused to provide ongoing services with this family, in spite of the fact the child clearly needs them.

Every time you schedule an appointment, or even a phone call to talk with the parent about payment and continuing services, you receive some excuse or explanation, but no money, and what's more alarming, no conversations. The parent is quite adept at blocking every effort you make. As you increase the written and verbal messages about the amount due, the parent begins to bemoan "discrimination," and "forcible pressure," and other words that have legal ramifications. Is this situation about fear? Is it about poverty and discrimination?

It's about power, and this parent is showing an expertise at manipulation, accusation, and self-proclaimed victimization. You will have to be the next organization in this child's life that has had to deal with a power player, and probably unsuccessfully, as far as the child's well-being goes. You can put it off and allow the situation to escalate up the Empowerment scale, or you can set up an action plan that meets every legal requirement your organization comes under to end services at a specific date. You might fall into the trap of getting frustrated or angry to meet this dominating parent. Or you can utilize other Empowerment emotions of courage and determination to execute a plan finally.

No more excuses or explanations.

A more complete view of the Emotional System of Empowerment is shown on the next page. The mild emotions are at the bottom, the moderate emotions are in the middle, and the intense emotions are at the top, with an arrow pointing up as intensity increases.

Emotions may not have a noticeable or significant amount of "feeling" at the time the emotion is engaged. Conventional thinking about anger, for example, is that the angry person is hot, loud, and forceful. But not always are angry people obviously angry. Sometimes they can be strategic, pointed, deceptive and perfectly calm in appearance. You might hear someone say, "I don't get angry. I get even."

At a mild level, this emotional system is more easily satisfied or resolved when some kind of power or control is gained, or a small change is accomplished. Not much energy is expended in accomplishing the drive of obtaining or having or possessing. At a moderate level, more energy will be put into the forceful change or domination. At a passionate level, excessive energy can be expended to control, force an outcome, or win.

RAGE
Fury
Bitterness
Contempt
Vehemence
Cynicism
Outrage-Violence
Exasperation
Revulsion
Courage

HATRED
Lust
Disdain-Pity
Aggression
Jealousy-Envy
Sarcasm
Indignation
Insult`
Boldness
Competitiveness

ANGER
Madness
Disgust
Meanness
Dismay
Resentment
Condescension
Selfishness
Frustration
Annoyance

UPSETNESS
Determination
Irritation
Unhappiness
Discontent
Pique-Peeve
Boredom-Apathy
Complacency
Tolerance

CALMNESS

What can I do about it? The Ladder Principle

Anger and all its teammates in the system of Empowerment are every-where in modern society. The desire and techniques for gaining power and control saturate our daily experience.

- You don't let someone into traffic, and they may explode with road rage—you're cautious about making eye contact or doing anything that would trigger that person

- The parent of one of your students or young customers comes storming at you to change a grade, make a refund, get hired, do what the parent demands, or else...

- Political divisions are at an all-time impasse, with either side using every power trick to destroy or overcome the other, and an increasing number of people just drop out of the entire process, too frustrated to participate

- Your neighbor comes screaming at you because your grass clippings blew over on his driveway

It's unrelenting. So, what can you do about it? Emotions slide up and down within their system, so the Ladder Principle is taking an action at an emotionally lower step, rather than waiting to act until the emotion is much more intense.

For example, instead of taking no action and expressing no emotion until a person hits Furious, develop and initiate an action and process of expression at Annoyance or Irritation. Decide the change or shift in power that you want to see as a resolution, then act earlier in the process, when your emotion is at a lower level.

If you are dealing with a person who is showing signs of increasing Empowerment emotions, work to provide an opportunity for that person to begin taking action or expressing their feelings at a stepped-down lower level.

Chapter 5

The Emotional System of Depletion and Its Co-Workers

The fourth emotional system is Depletion. This system includes the emotions of tiredness, sadness, grief, woundedness, and exhaustion. It is resolved when personal resources are replenished or healed. Consider some Storylines to illustrate this system.

Storyline 17: You have a colleague, a good friend, who works in a fairly sizable organization where you are a senior divisional manager. This friend works in Human Resources. The executive management decided it would be a great idea if HR conducted a two-day team-building "retreat" (they called it an "Advance") at a very high-end conference center, located in some mountains about one hundred miles away. They also decided unilaterally that HR would conduct the event. A very generous budget was provided so the team of four planners, headed by your friend, could "do it right."

The event was a spectacular success in every way imaginable. The Advance team spent about three hundred hours planning every detail, as part of their jobs in the company. Numerous details fell into place in the last day or two before the event occurred, pushing these four to their creative limits. And they pulled together and did it. At the event itself, your colleague was the Master of Ceremonies, a perfect fit for such an extroverted personality. Up on stage or coordinating team-building small group exercises through the twenty-two programmed hours, your friend certainly made a major positive impression on the bosses. The first day was 8 a.m. until 10 p.m., and the second day was 8 a.m. until 4 p.m., every minute having something to plan, to organize, or to execute.

The team was present at the retreat center the afternoon before everyone came and stayed until noon the day after everyone left, to do pre-brief, confirm every detail, and debrief. In every way, this was a spectacular event.

Two days after the event was all wrapped up, your friend quit the company.

Seriously? Why do people do that? That's just crazy.

Storyline 18: You love to ride bicycles. You have all the proper equipment and have ridden safely for many years. Out for a nice ride on Saturday you were tooling along in the bike lane, and some young kid in his parents' minivan came bolting backward down a driveway, not bothering to look for cars…or bikes!

You had just about three seconds to see the van backing up, clearly not stopping before crossing your lane right in front of you. You jammed the hand brakes on, and the front one caught tight. The bike flipped and you went over the handlebars, missing the van's rear end by inches and landing on the asphalt street. Bike's OK, but you're not. In addition to the terrible fright of a near accident, you got a nice four-inch cut on your left shoulder, requiring seven or eight stitches.

Before you left the scene, the kid's parent had heard the screech of the son's tires braking, and your thud hitting the ground hard. The kid, a seventeen-year-old boy, was crying and very upset, and your vicious anger at his utter stupidity and immature driving was melted by his tears. You just kind of sucked it up and exchanged insurance information. They even drove you to the emergency center and back again. You could ride home, albeit quite gingerly.

You had some things to do on Sunday, but you woke up exhausted. You could not pull it together to climb out of bed. A nice cup of coffee did nothing for you. It was really no big deal! You can't be utterly exhausted from one little cut. Can you?

You stayed in bed all day Sunday, and barely dragged yourself to work on Monday. What a baby! (You, in your own opinion.)

Storyline 19: Your neighbor next-door lost her husband of forty-eight years eight months ago. She's around seventy years of age, in very good health, has always been active around the neighborhood and in her yard. She and her husband apparently had a very warm relationship, several children, and a passel of grandchildren, none of whom live in the immediate area. You still see family in and out of the house on a regular basis. She hasn't been forgotten by family or friends.

However, over the past couple of months, as summer has turned to autumn, you notice she's not enthusiastic in returning your greeting. Sometimes, it takes a couple "Hello!" remarks before she looks up at you and responds with a tired, "Hi." You resolve that it's time for a good hot cup of neighborly coffee and a coffee cake. So, on a weekend morning when you know she'll be home, you load up your supplies and show up at her door.

"Coffee and coffeecake for what ails the soul!" you exclaim heartily when she opens the door to you. She invites you in, to the kitchen table, and everything is as neat as a pin there. She smiles weakly about the coffeecake and gets out cups and creamers that you both enjoy. After chit-chatting and sipping coffee, you ask as compassionately as possible, "So, how are you? You seem so…quiet these days."

Without tears, her sad eyes look at you and she says, "I don't think I've ever gotten over my husband's death. I don't think I ever will, not until I die too."

"Oh, no, you will," you insist with all the confidence you can project. "It just takes some time."

"My doctor says I'm probably depressed. I think I am depressed. He wants me to start on some mild antidepressants. I was brought up to think that a medication will never solve a problem, just cover it over. What do you think? Should I take an antidepressant?"

She looks at you for an answer.

Your turn. What do you say next? Why do people do this to you? You can't answer her problems for her and you certainly can't dispense medical advice. But, it's your turn.

This system, called Depletion, is fourth in random order, not because it is one of the last things a person thinks of feeling. These three Storylines all deal with varying intensities of Depletion emotions, from fairly mild to moderate to intensely passionate.

The System of Depletion is a scale of emotional responses linking interpreted perceptions to drives of resting, recovering, healing, and restoring.

Looking at the graphic of The Emotional System of Depletion on the following page, you can see eight emotional titles, moving from left to right and up the incline, which identify different intensities within this system. A person's emotional state will be very different based on his or her personal capacities in the many areas of life.

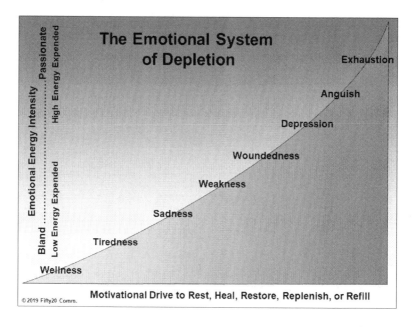

The concept of personal capacities is vital to a clear understanding of this emotional system. Imagine that your life is like a glass and imagine that it's filled right to the brim. You might say, "That never happens!" even before I explain the concept. From 12 midnight through one calendar day to 11:59 p.m. at the end of that 24-hour period, you have exactly one thousand, four hundred, and forty minutes in your glass, same as everybody. Your glass refills completely every stroke of midnight. (You smart alecks are bringing up time-change days in the spring and fall for Daylight Saving Time. Skip that.)

With regard to time, every human being has the same capacity every day. Immediately upon the stroke of midnight, you start using seconds—in fact, sixty of them every minute. They trickle out like soldiers marching in a line. Eighty-six thousand, four hundred of them, every day.

The human quality of capacities ends its universal equality in this glass. But wait, there's more! You have many glasses, all filled to varying levels of your individual capacity in that area. Every area of your perceptions, your relationships, your thinking, and your actions have variable capacities. Every day they change; perhaps even within a day they can change.

For example, I have a capacity for sound in my brain. If I am rested and the day has calm periods in it, I am not drained out by children playing around me or construction workers outside my office. I am not depleted by music playing. However, if I have to talk to someone, which is more draining to my mind than just listening, I find my capacity to listen is drained down, and I need some silence just to be able to process a simple thought. By the combination of listening and talking (putting thoughts into words), my capacity is drained down. What took me a long time to understand was when certain capacities in my life are drained down by normal use, it sucked capacity out of many other areas. With certain kinds of experiences I had, I was much more tired in a shorter time frame than with other kinds of experiences. That's what the system of Depletion, tiredness, and its co-workers is.

Let's take one more turn at the three Storylines that introduced this chapter.

Storyline 17: Your friend quit two days after the best "mountaintop" experience. Not only is that not surprising, everyone can plan on plummeting to a "depths of the pit" after soaring to the "heights of the sky." Your colleague is obviously one of the best in your company's HR department. He came through spectacularly at an event all the recipients thoroughly enjoyed. Your colleague spent way more energy, thought, personality, worry, and thrill in two days (plus the preparatory and debriefing times) than the other participants did in a month. Even in the few hours between closing down day one and launching day two, any sleep snatched did not provide a refilling of what was expended. Too much going on to rest at all.

One of the reasons many clergy take the day off after their Sabbath (whichever day that is in their tradition) to golf or fish or waste time at any other worthless activity is the need to recover from putting it all out there for the congregation.

Search out your exhausted friend, and graciously refuse to accept the resignation. Of course, it will help greatly if you can make some kind of investment that is restorative to your friend, like taking him or her out to their favorite lunch spot and buying lunch as a personal "thank you" for what you got out of the Advance. You can assure your friend that wanting to walk away from the car when it runs out of fuel is normal. A better plan than quitting outright when someone is that depleted is to take two or three personal refreshment days to do whatever restores the empty tanks.

If it's actually something else, deal with it. But if it's the dumps after the heights, it's normal. It's human. It's OK.

Storyline 18: You as a seasoned cyclist can diminish the overall effects of this incident. But look at all the draining factors in so many of your various glasses:

- You experienced the worst type of accident, one that could not in any way be anticipated or avoided. Your fright, as intense as it was, took a lot of energy out of you.

- Your anger at the stupid young driver, which you had to suck up when he started crying, took double energy. It's draining to get angry, and it takes more energy to suck that back up—you get no benefit from sucking up your own anger when it has to be done.

- You lost blood and skin. Not a lot, but your body has to replace that blood and rebuild that skin. Stitches do not heal. They only hold the split-open skin close enough edge-to-edge so it can knit back together. That's the healing. Be aware that in addition to the wound itself, your body has to:

- ○ fight a bunch of maniac germs and bacteria you picked up from the street,

- ○ get your vestibular and proprioceptive systems over the shock of flipping over the handlebars, and

- ○ process out of your body the Novocain the emergency room doctor shot into the wound to allow for stitches to be put in. Ouch!

• You have to remember the names of these new people you met inadvertently at the house, the hospital, the bystanders, a few other miscellaneous people. You like people, but meeting new ones is draining.

• Your perfect record of cycling without a major accident is now gone. How important is that to you? Giving that up, in your own mind, can be draining, if it's an important value to you.

So, with all that expenditure, it's no wonder that Sunday was a pull-the-covers-over-your-head day. Give it a rest.

Storyline 19: This situation is complicated. These are the big issues in life. A widow, after nearly fifty years of marriage, doesn't have the resources to resolve the grief. Who takes classes in preparing for grief recovery during those fifty years, before you need it?

That's not it. For this Storyline, some givens, which are not necessarily part of every grief journey, will help in illustrating my point in this system. You key in on the report from your older neighbor that her doctor suggested she might be depressed. She confirmed the possibility. She talked twice about antidepressants. That's a lot of uses of "depression."

A clinical psychological condition does exist called depression. It is an imbalance within the brain of certain chemicals that are necessary for a healthy brain to function properly. Since this woman's life circumstances seem to suggest an emotional depletion and not a biochemically-based clinical depression, try a different approach.

"So, you think you might be depressed," you suggest.

"Yes, I might be," she says, without a lot of conviction.

"Try telling me, 'I think I'm depleted.' Say that to me instead," you say. She says, "What? You want me to say, 'I'm depleted'"?

"Sure. Try it."

"I think I'm depleted, since my husband died."

"That's interesting. What tank in your life is emptied out, dried up?" you say comfortingly.

"Oh, I haven't been really hugged since my husband died. Oh, the little kiss-on-the-cheek and three-pats-on-the-back hugs I get. But not the good ones."

"Not even from your family members?" you ask.

"I think they might be afraid of hurting me more. They don't want me to miss him worse. But I need a different kind of hug. A real one," she offers tentatively. "And, I haven't laughed in a long time, since before my husband got sick there, right at the end. My 'laugh tank' is pretty empty."

OK, now you have something to work with. Everyone has lots of glasses with varying capacities, and some of those get drained out dry and the person starts the day dried out there. Even if the original capacity is a thimble-full, or a five-gallon bucket, regardless of the capacity, when the tank is dry, it's exhausting.

"Well," you say, "I'll give you a good hug when I leave, but I want you to try something. Talk to several of your most supportive family members and close friends and tell them how you want to be hugged by them. Tell them what 'a good hug' is for you. And ask them if they can give you one of those 'good hugs' every time they see you. And find one or two friends and rent some movies that have always made you laugh. Have them over to watch with you. Get some favorite snacks and laugh until your sides hurt. Can you try that?"

If you can find out which tanks are depleted in yourself or others, and develop a plan to replenish those empty tanks, you'll help with this system of Depletion.

There's nothing "good" about feeling depleted. Who wants to feel sad all the time?

Totally wrong thinking. Human beings are biological creatures, which unites us with rhythms of the entire world. As the world rotates on its axis in approximately twenty-four hours, it gets a daytime for growth and activity and a nighttime to rest and recover every day. As the world revolves around the sun approximately every 365.25 days, tipped at 23.5 degrees off center, the world gets a spring, a summer, an autumn, and a winter, in varying intensities, to grow, bear fruit, and rest. Our bodies respire moisture out and we become thirsty, needing water. Our body's cells use energy which must be consumed, stored, and replenished.

Our bodies are not invincible. When injured, the pain sensors alert us to the injury, warn us to protect the injured area, or outright stop us in our tracks. The goal of pain is not punishment; it is not intrinsically bad. Pain is to allow healing, to compel rest, to force a time to restore. Pain is a great aspect of our bodies, a benefit as surely as pleasure is. Both are necessary. Both are good.

Because human beings are relational and communal, we develop bonds that connect us to others, whom are trusted without hesitation and make a healthy life possible, especially for the very young, the very old, and the very weak. When the bonds and relationships we have are damaged or severed, the pain we experience has the same objective: to allow for rest, recovery, and replenishment.

Resolving Emotions of Depletion

Depletion emotions are not an absence of emotion, though sometimes one might feel listless, bland, or empty. These emotions have the presence of an energy working to ensure we are incited to rest, to stop, to find ways of replenishing what has been damaged or expended.

When a person is thirsty, and that person consumes an adequate amount of appropriate water in some form, the thirst is gone. Usually. Hunger is most often satisfied with consuming nourishing food. An injured part of the body is healed with rest and a recovery regimen. Usually.

Usually. But not always. Sometimes, a damage has occurred that is so profound, so deep, so overwhelming, that a simple formula of rest and recover does nothing to touch it. All of the systems can experience such extreme stress that resolution seems impossible. In such cases, care by a professional therapist, counselor, physician, or other expert in the field can recommend therapies and oversee processes that can help a deeply wounded or emptied person recover.

Post-Traumatic Stress Disorder (PTSD) is a relatively new term used to identify a personal wound so profound that ordinary processes don't work. Although PTSD is commonly associated with military service, it actually can result from any excessive stressor as perceived and interpreted by anyone, according to their own personal capacities.

Storyline 20: Fraternal twin ten-year-olds, a boy and a girl, have a pet cat. They saw this cat born, gave it a name, cared for it through its kitten years, and have the cat sleep with each one on alternating nights. They adore this cat.

Of the ten types of perception, the boy has particularly adept hearing, and his skin is especially sensitive to temperature and wetness. The girl has very alert vision, and notices tiny movements, many more colors than others see, and can already handle a tennis racquet well because the ball seems to come in slow motion over the net.

One day, the two children are playing in the front yard of their house, and of course, their cat is near them. A ball goes out in the road and the cat chases it. The boy and the girl start to intercept the cat, to keep it from the road, but they cannot reach it in time. A car hits the cat, violently and instantly killing it in front of the children. At the moment of impact, both children had looked away toward where they were running by the sidewalk. Both children heard the impact and heard the wail of the cat as it died. A tiny speck of the blood from the cat landed on the cheeks of both children.

It is possible that the boy may never get over the death of this pet, and struggle with PTSD for a long time, if not the rest of his life. He heard the cat die, and one of his most sensitive senses of perception is his amazing hearing. His sister also heard it, but she didn't actually watch the accident happen at the split second it occurred. That image is not in her memory. A tiny speck of blood splattered on both their cheeks. The girl didn't even feel it. The boy is hypersensitive to temperature and wetness, and that speck of blood is like being doused by a gallon of it. He cannot stop feeling it.

Both children experienced a great loss, for which they were not prepared at the moment or in life to that point. The girl may grieve and feel very sad for a long time. She may have great nostalgia about that cat. But its death will not redefine her life. The boy, her twin, suffered at a level where there are no words. He cannot talk about what he sensed, because human language cannot convey the true enormity of all the sounds he heard and all the sensations he felt.

Where a normal passage of time and common grieving practices allow the girl to heal, the boy may need extensive help in unraveling the sounds from the deepest part of his mind and resolving the wetness of that speck of blood he still can feel exactly on his cheek where it touched him.

Many soldiers come home, changed but unscathed, from the same battle experiences that left others with PTSD. How can two soldiers in the exact same environment come away from that experience in such profoundly different ways? Reality is never an absolute, something that exists. It is interpreted by our perceptions, which may have tremendous differences in sensitivity and capacity from one soldier to the next soldier within arm's reach. Their emotional makeup processes those perceptions differently, and their complexes of motivations and behaviors impact their awareness of reality. One can have damage to their soul in one day while a comrade in the same place and time doesn't even remember the day too clearly.

A more complete view of the Emotional System of Depletion is shown on the next page. The mild emotions are at the bottom, the moderate emotions are in the middle, and the intense emotions are at the top, with an arrow pointing up as intensity increases.

EXHAUSTION
Agony-Deadness
Despair
Anguish
Abandonment
Lostness
Brokenheartedness
Despondency
Ache
Grief

DEPRESSION
Draining
Woundedness
Sorrow
Dejection
Damage
Pain-Neediness
Emptiness
Pessimism
Loneliness

HURT
Abandonment
Weakness
Loneliness
Downheartedness
Forgetfulness
Confusion
Apathy
Ill-Sick
Doubt

SADNESS
Discouragement
Disappointment
Chagrin
Melancholy
The Blues-Blah
Tiredness
Complacency
Refreshment

WELL

Emotions do not flow in nice, neat, straight sequences, properly moving up or down this kind of scale in order. You might not include some of these words as aspects of Depletion at all, but only as a state of being and not a feeling. You may find that slang words or expressions are more common. It is that emotions fit together in a system, with similar factors and driving toward similar outcomes.

At a mild level, this emotional system is more easily satisfied or resolved when rest or refilling of the immediate need is received. At a moderate level, more energy will be put into ending the ongoing activity level, or whatever is draining the person's resources. At a passionate level, excessive energy will be expended to stop, to end, to recover.

What can I do about it?

When emotions in the Depletion realm occur, it is certain that the person feeling them perceives that he or she has become depleted, and is yearning for rest, recovery, or restoration. The most important question is, what action or inaction will restore the empty tanks in that person's life? What works? Is it a day off? A week? Quitting a job or a role? Some things can't be quite like that. Walk out on a relationship? Leave a neighborhood? It sometimes seems like there is no acceptable answer to this question.

A tool that is quite useful is The Question Sequence. In short form, it is:

1. Ask questions

2. Get answers

3. Ask better questions

I developed a list of seven kinds of questions that can be asked:

1. Inquiry – a yes, no, maybe so, I don't know question

2. Interrogative – requires an explanation, not a single word

3. Exploratory – looks for basic causes or outcomes

4. Investigative – analysis or synthesis of information

5. Hypothetical – possible or impossible potential alternatives

6. Rhetorical – a statement formed as a question

7. Dumb – an obvious, out-of-place, or surprising question

What makes a question a better question? If you imagine the subject you are facing as a fruit tree, when you ask the seven kinds of questions, you are going around and around the tree, looking at it from every angle, studying the details, getting lots of information. But a better question goes two ways:

1. Down into the roots

2. Up into the fruits

The roots of the subject at hand are delving into all the factors and issues that can pertain to the subject at hand. Where did this profound feeling come from? What started it? How long has it been besetting your life? Where are its roots?

The fruits of the subject at hand are considering how the current subject can play out in the long run. What's the life cost of letting this go on without resolution? What does it lead to, short-term and long-term? Where are you going with this issue?

Getting into roots and fruits changes the nature of the conversation or situation positively. Once you discover some of the roots, you can begin to develop resolutions that will affect the profound feelings which may tie into the person's perceptions, motivations, and behaviors as well.

Chapter 6

The Emotional System of Celebration and Its Neighbors

The fifth emotional system is Celebration. This system may also include the emotions of happiness, gratitude, excitement, thrill, and compulsion. It is resolved when a person gives, shares, shines, or spreads outwardly. Consider some storylines to illustrate this system.

Storyline 21: You and a woman friend are shopping in a mall. Because of an upcoming holiday, quite a crowd fills the large inner corridor. You and your friend are chatting about which store to hit next.

Your friend is a calm, quiet person, much like you in many ways. Neither of you seeks the spotlight and does not relish a lot of public attention lavished on you. You've known each other for years, and thoroughly enjoy the times you get to do things like this. Like normal people do, you keep an eye on the crowds milling about, just being aware of your surroundings.

Without warning, your friend screams a name very loudly, "Katie! Katie!" Your normally sedate and reserved associate is jumping up and down and gesturing wildly, across the mall open expanse. Every person in the area of the mall hears the commotion and makes a small effort to open a path for her to race across the crowded area to Katie, who has a huge smile on her face. And a huge belly to match! "She's *pregnant!*" your friend shouts loud enough for everyone within one hundred yards to hear. Everyone smiles at the exuberance.

Your friend makes a beeline to the surprised Katie, and they throw their arms around each other and dance back and forth for a few seconds. You finally catch up to them, and your normally subdued and conservative friend proudly proclaims, "Katie's *pregnant!* Can you believe it?" Katie is smiling, but a little embarrassed at the fuss.

You can believe it, of course. But why would someone make such a big deal about a baby on the way?

Storyline 22: You have been invited to the birthday party of a three-year-old, the first child of a young couple you know. You are one of the earliest guests to arrive. You had purchased a very nice gift that is age-appropriate for this little 1,095-day old person. Your gift is beautifully wrapped in a sizable box, with colorful paper and a bright ribbon. You carry the present in the backyard to put on the gift table, but the child and one parent are right there. Instead of unceremoniously adding your delightful offering to the growing pile on the table, you kneel to eye-level and give the gift directly to the child. With very evident happiness, the child looks up at the parent and asks, "Can I open it now? Can I? Can I?"

The parent calmly responds, "What do you say?" The child says nothing.

The parent has a slight warning tone in addressing the child by name, "Come on now. What do you say?" The child looks at the parent, then at you, and says nothing. "You don't get a gift if you don't say, 'Thank you.' Say 'Thank you!'" The child says nothing.

The parent is now somewhere between embarrassment toward you and annoyance toward this little person who has had one actual birth day and two more celebrations of that day, none of which are remembered. "Say 'Thank you' right now, or I'm taking this present away." The child looks at the parent, not at you, and says, "Thank you."

"Not to me!" the parent exclaims. The parent takes the gift out of the child's hands, and the child tears up, with a pouting mouth and trembling lower lip. "Thank you," this little confused recipient mumbles.

"That's not sincere. You're not really grateful for this gift, are you?" scolds the parent. To you, your 9,225-day old friend says apologetically, "I'm so sorry!"

You lamely say, "That's alright. Kids have a hard time saying, 'Thank you.'"

The child looks at you and says nothing.

You're actually right, but possibly for the wrong reason. Some kids have a hard time expressing gratitude. They love to take gifts, but don't like to say "Thanks" unless forced to. But why do they do that?

Storyline 23: If you knew you couldn't be hurt, what would be the most thrilling thing you would try that you've never done before?

- Jump out of an airplane at thirty thousand feet…without a parachute, aiming for a huge flex-net set up with about one hundred feet of clearance to the ground

- Ride every roller coaster in the world in one year, just over 1,400 or about four per day, ending with Outlaw Run at Silver Dollar City in Branson, Missouri, never touching a safety bar with your hands

- Swim with the sharks at New Smyrna Beach, Florida, the most dangerous beach in the world, without a cage

- Talk back directly to your boss, using the nickname everyone calls him behind his back

- Park your ten-year-old minivan in your garage, not wearing your seatbelt

- Add your own thrill option here

Of course, you know the proposal is impossible. You can get hurt tying your shoes, and you're likely to be the only person who misses that net by ten feet to the left. So, you always play it safe. But there's a guy in your work area, in a cubicle three over and two down, who lives for thrill. He always has a new story about some hair-raising, high-risk activity he did last weekend. This guy drives like a maniac who thinks he's at the Indianapolis 500 speedway instead of on the six-lane headed to boring work. Occasionally, he checks his own social media account, during scheduled breaks, of course, and reviews his exciting adventures, punctuating the air with a whoop and a whistle.

He is a show-off, in your opinion. How can anybody compete with a guy like that? How does he keep it up? Is he faking it?

The fifth system is called Celebration. These three Storylines all deal with varying intensities of Celebration emotions, from fairly mild to moderate to intensely passionate. In the three anecdotes presented above, you and the other participants in the scenes are dealing with different expressions and intensities of this system.

The System of Celebration is a scale of emotional responses linking interpreted perceptions to drives of sharing, giving, shining, or spreading out.

Looking at the graphic of The Emotional System of Celebration below, you can see eight emotional titles, moving from left to right and up the incline, which identify different intensities within the emotional system of Celebration. A person's emotional state will be very different based on opportunity, personality style, and many other variables.

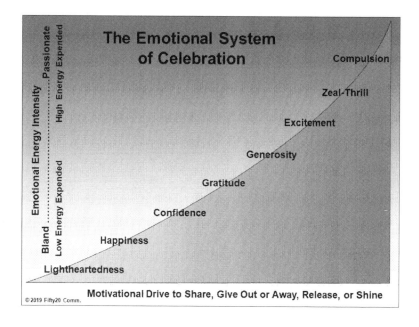

It can be very challenging to separate an emotional state or experience from a personality trait or an attitude. Is generosity a "feeling" in the system of Celebration, or a decision based on values one holds or resources one possesses? It probably is not necessary to separate into exclusive camps the concepts of emotion and character any more than one can truly separate the human cardiovascular system from the respiratory system. In theory, to learn better about each aspect of our body, we can consider one part of our intertwined design as separated from another one. But in the reality of life itself, they are inseparable, functioning simultaneously and interdependently.

Let's look at the three Storylines of this chapter with attention given to the Celebration aspects.

Storyline 21: As you might suspect, there's a few parts of this story you don't know yet. Once your calm, normally conservative friend has introduced you to Katie, Katie explains that they are old, old friends having grown up together, through some pretty tough times. She had a serious infection requiring several surgeries. As a result of many complex circumstances, Katie had lost a number of pregnancies. Every time she was going through this trauma, her solace and comfort was calling her "dear sister," who is your friend, now so choked up she can't even talk. They talked for hours about the loss, the pain, the hope Katie still clung to. Your friend was her rock in the storms of life.

Your quiet friend's exuberance is an intense form of Celebration. She shares her joy loudly and vocally, with a rising tone in her voice, a broad smile on her face, her arms thrown outwardly, her feet racing across the mall corridor. She shines in every possible way. She does not care who sees or hears her; in fact, she wants everyone to see and hear her. This is no ordinary pregnancy—it is a gigantic victory. Katie wanted to be absolutely sure she had surpassed the number of weeks at which she had lost the previous pregnancies, and she was set to call her dear friend later that evening with the incredible news. This baby was going to make it! But the mall meeting happened first.

Storyline 22: You might think I am just throwing in the number of days the parent and the child have been alive as a cute statistic, but it is to make an important point. The exactly-to-the-day three-year-old has virtually no memory of previous birthdays. This little person has a budding vocabulary appropriate for his or her age, largely formed of one- or two-syllable words. The 9,225-day-old is roughly twenty-five years and three months old, with eight times more experience than the child. In the system of Celebration, the child has probably gotten the feeling of "happy" down pretty well, but "gratitude," "generosity," and "excitement" are words never before used by a three-year-old, and certainly not understood yet.

The child is a concrete thinker, not primarily using language yet for thoughts of the moment. A child this age uses images, visible and tangible objects. A book about a farm for a three-year-old has pictures of specific animals, buildings, and machinery. It will picture plants by the food eaten from it, and never mention planning strategies, crop rotations, organic fertilizers, or farm bureau loan policies. Say "cow," and the child has a picture in mind. Say "thank," and no picture is possible. A young child once was told to pick up his room. After an hour, the parent who had issued the order came in and found nothing picked up at all. The parent was furious and asked why the room was not picked up. The child, not wanting to disappoint, could not figure out how to grab a corner of the room and pick it up. It was too big. He thought literally to pick up the room, not put dirty clothing into a basket and place toys in the toy box.

You are right to be aware that young children have a hard time saying, "Thank you," not because they are inherently selfish or greedy or rude. It is because they are so concrete in their thinking that any word not having a specific image it produces has no meaning to their minds. The parent is talking way above the child's experience and has expected an emotional response that is not within that child's vocabulary yet.

The parent is the better equipped person to express and demonstrate simple gratitude, which the child can watch, learn, and emulate. Perhaps even this year, but certainly over the next couple years, an expressive, grateful parent will lead a child to become expressive and grateful. A rude and demanding parent will produce…oh, well, you get it.

Storyline 23: Does an extrovert have a more thrilling life than an introvert? That probably is a matter of personal opinion. Persons who have an outgoing personality fit more naturally into the emotions we find in the Celebration system. An experience that may be perceived as thrilling to one person, such as riding in a race car going 180 mph on a test track, may be terrifying to another person. Finishing a one thousand-piece puzzle successfully may cause one person to rejoice and pump their fists into the air in victory, while another person cannot imagine anything more boring.

A naturally quiet and internal person in a connection or relationship to a loud, outgoing person may need a translator, if not an arbitrator, to be able to understand and work with each other. Both ends of the spectrum of Celebration are valid, and neither is "better" than the other intrinsically.

The Problem with "You Make Me So Happy"

Conventional thinking makes happiness a prime goal in life, if not the ultimate goal. One challenge in our culture is to define what "happiness" actually is. The Declaration of Independence of the United States includes as a given that all human beings have "certain unalienable rights, that among these are Life, Liberty and the pursuit of Happiness." So, what is the Happiness that we have a right to pursue? In the eighteenth century, "Happiness" was understood as prosperity, well-being, or the accumulation of possessions that ensures a good life. In the modern day, Happiness is pleasure, or needs satisfaction. It commonly is defined as "something that makes me happy." That implies, if not actually defines, the source of happiness as external to a person.

This presumption is common in all the five emotional systems. A person's personal state, frame of mind, and emotional response is thought of as an external process, not an internal one. The relationship of the four complexes—perceptions, emotions, motivations, and behaviors—is personal and internal. One cannot shed the privileges and responsibilities of owning these aspects. Though it might seem like a meaningless play on words, the two statements below are not at all equal.

"I feel happy when eating a chocolate bar."

"Chocolate makes me happy."

The first statement takes ownership for the emotions associated with the activity, with the external stimulus. The second statement shifts ownership for the emotions out of the person and onto the object. The process of experience is that the chocolate is a stimulus, a complex carbohydrate that contains a bitter extract of a particular bean, mixed with a variety of sweeteners and sugars, designed to have a certain effect in the mouth. When seen, smelled, touched, or tasted, chocolate affects multiple senses simultaneously, and a chocolate lover's response may include desire, pleasure, and satisfaction at many levels. The motivation is to eat the chocolate, and the behaviors include holding it and consuming it.

Emotional accuracy means each person can understand how his or her emotions function. Relinquishing the origin or control of one's own emotions to something or someone else prevents both emotional accuracy and emotional resolution. The expression "You make me so …" (fill in the blank with any emotional state, such as "happy," or "angry") creates a mental concept that the other person or thing has the ability and privilege to control the speaker. It also sets up a second concept, that the speaker has no absolute responsibility for his or her own emotions, and thus for the motivations and behaviors that link to them.

Can human beings interacting with others momentarily or in extensive patterns influence one another? Of course—that's the nature of relationships. Can one person "push the buttons" of another person, suspecting or knowing that a certain response is either likely or virtually guaranteed? That sequence is not only possible, it is common in human relationships. In benign forms, this development of building expectations is called "friendship." In abusive forms, this same development of building expectations is called "grooming."

In the Storyline below, I am assigning gender to the various participants. In part, the predator is depicted as male and the prey is female because this dynamic is very common. But always bear in mind that any actual Storyline can have a male or a female as the predator, of any age, in any kind of relationship to the prey, who can be male or female, of any age.

Storyline 24: Where you work, you have a regular but minimal professional contact with a man in a supervisory position. Your role in the organization is not placed within this individual's authority. You are basically a peer of his in a different department. For reasons you do not fully understand clearly, you are uncomfortable when in the presence of this man. You can't quite put your finger on why, but it is clear to your instinctive awareness about people that this person is dangerous. Of course, no one can be fired or demoted because someone else has a vague discomfort around that person.

You decide to increase your awareness about this man, whenever you have opportunity to be in his vicinity. You begin to notice and make a mental note of a number of behaviors produced by this man that, individually, seem benign, almost nice, but collectively give a foundation to your discomfort. Here are some of your observations:

1. This man stands about 50 percent closer to individuals who appear to be subordinate to him, standing taller and more face forward toward such an individual, and he seems to stand farther and more turned away from peers or superiors. He lingers around the weaker persons and moves away from stronger people.

2. Whatever he says to one of the weaker people, he tends to say more quietly, so that the person with whom he is speaking leans toward him to hear his words, even if very slightly. Usually, it is some kind of pleasant or funny conversation, because the prey individual smiles or laughs at his comments.

3. He discovers preferences held by certain prey individuals, such as what brand of beverage that person prefers, or what kind of music. The predator has a supply of that exact brand or knows some interesting story about a band in that genre, and provides that information pleasantly, which produces a delight response in the prey person.

4. This man has some prestige among many of the individuals in the organization because of his position, title, and ability. He is very good at what he does. You notice he makes eye-to-eye contact with certain prey individuals, one at a time, with a very slight wink or nod toward them. These glances might last two to three seconds, just a little longer than normal eye-to-eye contacts happen, which is about three-quarters of a second. The prey person smiles or shows some kind of enjoyment at the attention. This predatory man does not make eye contact with equals or superiors except for less than one-half second, and then he glances away.

5. This man seems to be constantly scanning the territory for prey individuals. He makes a particular effort to greet and learn the names of newcomers to the organization. He has a little gift or company pen to give, to inspire gratitude in the recipient. Prey individuals seem to feel special around him, while peers and superiors sense distrust or caution around him.

6. He makes a regular practice of initiating some kind of physical touch with prey individuals, always "appropriate" in the situation, but it's a common event. It could be as innocent as a handshake in greeting that lasts just a little longer than you would shake hands, or he reaches out with his left hand to touch further up the forearm or on the shoulder of the prey person. He has a wide variety of other contact points with prey persons, such as tousling their hair, or touching their back near

the backbone, or further up the arm toward the biceps. He makes regular use of alliance gestures like fist bumps or high fives with prey persons, to which that person smiles and seems happy to have a friend who is so powerful and respected.

7. Whenever a prey person seems to become uncomfortable or cautious around this man, he moves further away, stops the little gifts, avoids touching that person, and moves them into the peer or superior group. He never forces himself on anyone. It almost seems like playful teasing, finding out which prey person welcomes being special and enjoys that status, especially because it's private—just between the prey and the predator.

One day, the man is gone. Word around the organization is that he was arrested for sexual abuse with one of the youngest staff members, a seventeen-year-old high school graduate who began working there in the summer. She had told him she was nineteen, above the age of consent, but she was not. In the weeks that follow his arrest, she is one of his staunch defenders, not his accuser. She was thrilled to be the object of his attention. She was excited to come to work and was grateful for everything he did for her. Because of her naivete and inexperience in the world, she magnified the meaning of the little presents and her favorite snacks he provided. As the incidental little touches he initiated with her were not avoided, then reciprocated, he slowly advanced them, always watching for her to withdraw or become uncomfortable. When she didn't, he knew he had found his prey. That's how predatory manipulation can work.

He manipulated her system of Celebration so that she eventually plunged herself into a relationship, not based on love and desire but on thrill and extreme happiness. Can't anyone understand he just wanted to "make her happy"?

Resolving Emotions of Celebration

Celebration emotions provide the internal drive to spread oneself out, to give, to be generous and thankful. In extroverted individuals, the circumstances that stimulate feelings in this system may be very different than what stimulates an introvert. Some persons will be far more demonstrative and expressive about their perceptions, feelings, drives, and behaviors than others.

On the next page is a more complete list of emotions within the system of Celebration. The mild emotions are at the bottom, the moderate emotions are in the middle, and the intense emotions are at the top, with an arrow pointing up as intensity increases.

Some concepts and the words used to identify them can be placed in more than one system. For example, "trust" can be a moderate aspect of Acceptance, that a person allows access by someone to come toward him or her, to receive that person or situation. "Trust" also could fit in the system of Celebration, that allows an individual to step out into a person or situation, propelled outwardly by a feeling of confidence or enthusiasm.

What is important is to see the connections between perceptions to motivations and behaviors through the emotional systems. Because you might understand "trust" as an aspect of love and Acceptance does not mean everyone will use that word to mean that understanding. A rigid fixing of these words and the concepts they represent may result in a lowered understanding and awareness of reality as interpreted by yourself or someone else.

COMPULSION
Ecstasy-Mania
Exuberance
Arrogance
Pride
Zeal
Thrill-Craziness
Courage
Confidence-Faith
Gregariousness-Outgoing

EXCITEMENT
Enthusiasm
Delight-Elation
Ambition
Loyalty
Joy
Silliness-Giddiness
Laughter
Cheer-Humor
Hopefulness

GLADNESS
Generosity-Altruism
Empathy
Compassion
Relief
Thankfulness-Gratitude
Pleasure
Optimism
Consideration
Amusement

HAPPINESS
Connection
Lightheartedness-Fun
Peace
Contentment
Kindness
Easygoing
Carefree
Privacy-Quietness

GOODNESS

What can I do about it?

One conversational dynamic you can notice in yourself and in others is the tendency for each person in a conversation to be formulating his or her own next response, rather than actually listening to whoever is speaking at the moment. If one person is telling a story about a wonderful aspect of his or her family, life, travels, work, or ability, others in the conversation will be visibly preparing themselves to take the floor, relate their own stories that usually are "better" in some way, and "shine" brighter than the speaker. This phenomenon happens whether the story being told is a delightful aspect or a difficult one, such as an illness, a medical procedure, an accident, or some other challenging situation. Someone else always has a worse story to grab the limelight. You can listen.

Listen without developing an agenda to have a better story, a more exciting experience, or a more tragic outcome. When the person who is speaking pauses, prompt him or her with a question or statement that allows the storyteller to shine a bit more brightly, fill in some gaps, be the star for a moment. A neighbor of thrill and excitement is gratitude, and you will be amazed that the storyteller will experience sincere thanks to you when you enable that person to shine a little brighter.

Chapter 7

The Capacity Scale & Wrap-Up

People attempt to comfort others experiencing some kind of trauma with a few quips that are actually philosophies of life:

"God won't give you more than you can handle."

"Whatever doesn't kill you makes you stronger."

"You've got big shoulders—you can get through this problem."

These pithy one-liners usually don't actually bring much comfort to the afflicted. They cannot be proven as factual. Where the strength of a steel bar can be tested in a laboratory under very controlled circumstances, to determine at what pressure that particular steel buckles, a human being cannot be subjected to such a scientific approach for discovery.

In Chapter 5, the variable concept of capacity was introduced briefly. This concept is extremely important and applies to all aspects of all ten senses of perception, all five emotional systems, all dynamics of motivation, and all behaviors. The human being is limited. Period. So far as we can determine at this time, an infant's capacity to remember or use words to communicate is zero. Some individuals with a brain disease or injury also have a memory capacity of zero. A man or woman with severe dementia will live in the moment, literally. From one second to the next second, such an individual has no recall of the previous moment. This person may be very aware of what is seen and felt right now, but not be able to process the experience or recall it in any way.

The issue is about diminished capacity.

Other individuals may have learned multiple languages fluently and been able to utilize thirty thousand words in each of several of them. An individual with tremendous verbal capacity may have in mind up to two hundred thousand words. But there is the limit for that person. He or she has a limited capacity, even when it is a huge capacity. This principle of the limitations of capacity is absolute, to the point we might call it The Law of Limited Capacity.

Thus, the Law of Limited Capacity then also applies to human emotional systems. A necessary limit exists as to how much a person can crave or fear. There is a capacity to how angry a person can get, or how wounded an individual can feel. I am not referring to theoretical human capacity; I am referring to any particular individual's capacity. I realize that unusually gifted runners can cover a mile distance in under four minutes. The current record for one mile is 3:43.13, set in 1999, or approximately 16 mph. Though new time records may be set regularly, by tenths or hundredths of a second over the last record, no human being can run for one mile at twenty miles per hour, covering a mile in three minutes.

But I cannot run a mile in twelve minutes!

The fact is that one man out of all human beings who ever lived (and had their times officially recorded) can run a mile in 3:43.13, and the stark reality is I am not that man. My capacity is much more reduced. I am not trying to discover human limits of capacity, but my own limits of capacity. That's what really matters in a person's life.

Any particular individual may encounter a single experience, a set of experiences, or an entire personal culture that is beyond his or her capacity to feel or resolve. Any of the five emotional systems can engage a trauma or a stress for which that individual does not have the capacity to deal with. What happens in such a case? "What doesn't kill you…" speaks of the trauma or stress being reduced below the limits of capacity. "…makes you stronger" speaks of the capacity being enlarged. So, either the stressor decreases or the capacity increases.

But what if that doesn't happen? The stressor increases beyond capacity.

Consider these Storylines to explore this principle:

Storyline 25: A woman is raped by a man. It does not matter if she knew him previously or had never met him before that moment. In considering the principle of limited capacity, whether she fought back or passively submitted has no relevance. We will not consider if he was arrested, tried, convicted, and incarcerated to the limits of the law, or that he never got caught. The principle is not affected if the rape happened decades ago in another place and time, or if it happened within the last twenty-four hours in her most secure environment. None of that matters. The key is what this particular woman's personal capacity is to deal with, think about, feel through, and resolve the trauma of being raped. What any other woman could do, might do, would do, should do, or did do is irrelevant. Was this single event of a rape beyond the capacities of this particular woman?

Although more than one system can be engaged, for the purpose of illustration of a principle, let's consider her primary emotional response to all of her combined perceptions hit her limit in just one of the systems.

- Was she pushed beyond all of her capacity to love and receive someone, beyond an obsession with the traumatic experience as the defining moment of her identity?

- Was she terrified beyond the point of thinking or imagining how completely unsafe she is, and always will be?

- Was she driven beyond a rage so profound that no amount of violence she produces will ever change her history or her future?

- Has she been wounded in her soul and heart so deeply that she feels cleft in two, and she will never be whole again?

- Was she driven to an ecstasy of experience that is beyond her words, that makes every other experience of her entire life pale and lifeless in comparison?

Once she is beyond her capacity to feel, but the trauma does not abate and her capacity does not increase, where does the emotion go, when it has to go somewhere? It will go somewhere, but where?

Storyline 26: A man formed a company with his best friend from high school and college, developing a manufacturing process that was extremely successful and profitable. The genius in the process was his partner's. The genius in marketing and business was his. These two buddies had an incredible thing going, and great teamwork between them made it happen. All the employees, vendors, customers, and community benefited greatly. The families were intertwined in every area of life.

One Monday morning, this man went to his office and was shocked when he opened the door. Absolutely everything was gone. Everything. The machinery, the desks, the computers, the people. He couldn't catch his breath. He thought he might be having a heart attack or was in the worst possible nightmare of his life. Woodenly, he shut the door, stood for a second, and reopened the door to see if he had just made a mistake.

He hadn't.

He just stood there for a very long time. His wife, having been simultaneously warned of "the change" by the now-former partner's spouse, pulled in behind him, crying her eyes out. She stood beside him in the empty room, in utter shock as well. A couple of years ago, this genius partner began to realize how much more money he could make if he created a new company without his colleague. The processing system he had developed was his bright idea. Marketing and business were the easy parts. So, over many months, this trusted, lifelong friend hatched a plan to form a secret new company in another state. He siphoned off money through a complex array of dealings and connections. This evil genius even arranged for his unsuspecting partner and his wife to "win" a fabulous weekend getaway at a B&B about one hundred miles away. He had fallen for that too.

In addition to the processes and the equipment, this partner had sweet-talked the best employees into a new deal, promising all kinds of benefits and salary increases. This man was left with a huge lease on a now-empty facility. He had no processes. He had no employees. He had no resources. In one second (actually about five minutes), he became aware that everything he valued, except the woman who stood at his side, was gone. Unrecoverable.

How does he feel, even weeks or months after the "Big Slip," as he referred to it, happened? Numb. He feels nothing. No love. No fear. No anger. No pain. No joy. Nothing.

Storyline 27: A middle-aged man worked with a younger male co-worker. Both men are "family men," and they talk about their spouses and children regularly. Even though they are from different generations, they have socialized together and consider themselves friends. Their jobs require them to accomplish projects cooperatively, which they have done very well for several years. Together, they have brought their department some commendations, and they are very proud of their accomplishments.

One day, an electrical short in a large piece of equipment caused a fire in their work area. The initial explosion knocked the young man out, his head bleeding. The older man happened to be on the side of the fire that had a clear escape, but the younger colleague was trapped in an area with no door or window. While other workers escaped or attempted to knock down the fire, the older man made repeated attempts to reach under or around the blaze to grab his friend. At one point, he was able to get a hold of the younger man's arm, but lost his grip trying to pull him along the floor to safety. The fire intensified briefly, and incoming first responders dragged this valiant hero out to safety. The younger man died where he lay.

A valiant hero. The older man was immediately hailed as the "valiant hero" for his repeated attempts to save his co-worker. He got interviewed on television news programs, and a nice story was written about him. He got a commendation from the company. He got congratulations and respect everywhere he walked in the company.

He utterly hated it. All of it.

The more recognition he got, the angrier he became, until anger was about the only emotion he felt. Occasionally, he sensed he was verging on rage, and on rare days, his mood soured up to bitter annoyance. After about four years, his company ordered him to sign up for an anger management program.

It didn't work.

He's still angry to this day. Why would a hero be so angry?

When Emotions Are Not or Cannot Be Resolved

In many people's lives, even strong emotions can be resolved. The emotion is completed by connecting with a person's motivational complex, and the resulting behaviors bring about a positive result, relative to the purpose of the emotion. Love draws the desired person or object in. Anger brings change. Wounds cause rest and healing. Generosity inspires giving something away. It all works.

But it does happen that for a particular person, a single event, a series of experiences, or even the entire culture in which that person lives creates a trauma so great, the emotions driven by it don't work. They don't connect to the right values and habits. No actions bring a satisfactory outcome. The feelings intensify, and still are unproductive, unresolvable.

The very nature and experience of reality has undergone a radical reinterpretation because of the trauma. What might not be life-altering trauma for one person completely redefines what is perceived as real to another. The system of emotion which is central in the traumatic event cannot contain the energy expended. Words run out. Feelings run out. But the pressure of the event or total situation continues to build. The objective of the emotion cannot be achieved. It cannot be altered to another outcome. And it cannot be abandoned. The emotion expands beyond the limits of the original system, and beyond the capacity of the person to manage it. The excessive emotion comes out somewhere else. The title I use for this phenomenon is Topping Out.

When the energy expended toward resolution from one system resurfaces in another system, it takes on the general characteristics of the second system, but usually in an odd way. It might appear to be an expression of the second emotional system, but it's somehow not quite right. And resolutions that are effective in the second system do not resolve the topped-out emotion from the first system.

Let's reconsider the three Storylines above, particularly giving attention to the concept of topping out.

Storyline 25: The violation of rape is violently destructive to countless aspects of the victim. Certainly, the emotional systems of Exposure, Empowerment, and Depletion are engaged, but not equally by all rape victims in all circumstances. One of those three may become the dominant system as her response to reality as she perceives and interprets it. She may become so terrified that panic attacks occur with terrible frequency. She may experience a singular phobia or numerous phobias. Her anxiety may spread from locational safety to financial safety or intellectual safety or spiritual safety issues. She may eventually run out of any room in the Exposure system to feel any more. But she cannot stop the feelings from exploding.

This same concept can be repeated in the Empowerment or Depletion systems, with anger, insolence, and rage, or sadness, grief, or pain that is unrelenting. And the emotion keeps exploding.

So, they surface in another system. For the point of this illustration, extreme emotions from Exposure do not top out into Empowerment or Depletion. The energy forces an outlet in the Acceptance system. This victim of rape becomes promiscuous, sleeping around with virtually any man she can entice into bed. It is never enjoyable and creates no bonding. Often, the situation is dangerous. She cannot stop herself from being revictimized by predatory men. It's "love," but in an odd way. It doesn't seem right.

Or, the explosive energy tops out into the Celebration system. The rape victim becomes a comedienne, but with a mean twist. She becomes a talker, can't stop dominating most conversations. She gives every appearance of being a super extrovert, life of the party, top sales agent, go-getter. But she's never happy about anything. Always more pressure to give, go, get. She's outgoing, but it doesn't seem quite right.

Storyline 26: Sometimes, topping out results in an absence of emotion, in all five systems. This might be when the trauma produces explosive Empowerment emotion that surfaces as extreme Depletion, a numbness which is appropriate when a severe injury has happened, such as shock setting in to prevent the brain from experiencing overwhelming pain.

This businessman had trusted his partner at an extremely high level, bonding his very identity into the relationship with someone who eventually revealed himself as a sociopath. His former partner had no ability to empathize with others, to give even scant thought to others' feelings or issues. The man who got taken was a numbers guy, understanding easily the nature of marketing and selling, but not really grasping the human side of the equation.

When the partner stole all the stuff of the business, he absconded with one irreplaceable reality: the identity of his former partner. The real problem is, that identity disappeared with the theft. The man at the center of this story cannot find himself, and without a self, he has no emotions. His bank account, and his heart, are equally empty.

Storyline 27: The valiant hero truly does not believe himself to be a hero of any kind. He actually senses his fingertips gripping the cloth of his colleague's hot garment, and the sensation of it slipping out of his grasp is always present. He can actually feel it. A hero wins. A hero saves. A hero comes through for his friend.

He failed. And it cost his friend his life.

In his mind, the awful, horrible death of his friend is entirely his fault. He should not have gotten an award or a commendation. He should have gotten a trial for murder. No, more than that. He should have been the one who died in the fire. The younger man had his best years ahead of him, not behind him. Everything in the world now is upside down, inside out. And nothing he can ever do will make it right.

Because of all the attention showered on him as "the valiant hero," this man was not able to grieve for his profound losses. He is depleted beyond words, and he never had a chance to identify his pain, express it in any way, or heal from it. There was no rest for the weary.

Eventually, his exploding feelings of Depletion exceeded the entire system in his life, way beyond words. He wasn't a big one on talking anyway, and often stumbled over finding the right word he wanted. So, the anguish began to resurface in Empowerment, but in a very unhealthy way. For some inexplicable reason, he relished causing pain to others—that was his lot in life, he sadly concluded. He became nasty, belligerent, rude, insolent. He had an uncontrollable drive to control everything and everyone, to the destruction of most of his ordinary relationships.

He worked on his anger. He went to the anger management therapies. He read books about fixing anger. He meditated. He prayed. He tried everything, except addressing the actual roots of the anger. The anger was venting out through Empowerment, but the energy for it was from Depletion. If he were to process this profound sadness and grief that had become years old, his anger would subside, eventually drawing down the energy in the Empowerment system. It would drop in its energy drive to the point that it would appear as overwhelming anguish and pain. But at that point, he would actually be getting somewhere through the healing process. It might appear worse to be that crushed, but it's not. No expression of the anger, no momentary change would salve the wounds of his soul. Taking ownership of this life-altering moment that resulted in the death of his colleague and young friend will begin the long-sought healing process.

Resolving Topped-Out Emotions

In one of the buildings in which I have worked, the roof leaked. Mysterious brown spots appeared on the ceiling panels, revealing the sad presence of dripping water that made its way through the roofing, the insulation, and the steel panels. The steel panels, which form the foundation of the flat roof, were corrugated and welded along all the seams. The corrugations made countless little troughs, down which rainwater that had seeped through a crevice somewhere could make a run for it. Eventually, the water found a way out of the corrugated run and dripped on a ceiling panel below.

This flaw in the roof apparently had caused consternation for previous owners. Over the years, someone had tied plastic buckets in the rafters where drips had occurred. It seemed impossible to trace the original source of the incoming water, and it was impossible to fix the entire roof every time watermarks appeared on a ceiling tile.

That's kind of the way topped-out emotions work. Damage or excessive feelings in one area cannot work their way out in that system. The emotion builds up beyond the capacity of the person to manage it, much less resolve it. So it slides over to another system, and masquerades as that second emotion.

Tracking down the original source of topped-out emotions is not impossible, but it can be very difficult. It might be a task a person can approach and accomplish alone, but usually counseling or intense therapy is especially helpful.

The key to resolution is found in discovering the original unsolved traumatic source, and the excessive emotions that could not or were not addressed and resolved. Rather than focus the efforts of discovery and determination on the apparent emotional system, the resolution will come through the root emotional system.

One Final Tool You Can Use: The Vocabulary Choice

Language is the common means by which we think and process our perceptions, emotions, motivations, and behaviors. We put ideas into words, and the words we choose have tremendous impact on how we think, and once spoken, how the situations of life progress.

There are four verbs to avoid. At least listen for them, from your own mouth and from others:

1. Need

2. Should

3. Ought

4. Must

A few additional expressions mean the same thing: supposed to, have to, got to, or their slang counterparts. All four verbs are used excessively by teachers, preachers, politicians, parents, influencers, leaders, and just about everyone everywhere all the time. Listen for them, especially how often these four verbs become the main verb of the sentence.

"Need, should, ought, and must" are verbs of intended obligation. They press the hearers toward some desired or demanded action. The use of "need, should, ought, and must" is to convey importance, urgency, pressure, and threat of consequences. But most often, in practical terms, they mean nothing at all.

The first time I was impressed with the emptiness of these four verbs was at an organization's executive board meeting, in which I served as one of the department heads. A colleague, another department's leader, presented a plan for the upcoming year's focus in his department. His list included ten points:

1. We must enter...

2. We must develop...

3. We must change...

4. We must connect...

5. We must invade...

6. We must invent...

7. We must learn...

8. We must invest...

9. We must alter...

10. We must plan...

The other executives in the meeting all nodded approvingly and were impressed. The chair of the meeting asked a fateful question: Does anyone have any questions about this department's proposal?

Foolishly, I raised my hand.

Called on, I said to my colleague, "What do you mean we *must* do all these initiatives? What do you mean by the word 'must'"?

He said, "Well, we need to do these things."

I said, "What does 'need' mean? Are these actual needs we have?"

He said, "Well, we just have to do them. We ought to be doing all of them."

I said, "What do you mean by, 'We ought to do them?' What standard sets the obligation that demands we ought to invest in these ten focal areas?"

Everyone in the room seemed to have stopped breathing. No one ever questioned another department head's initiatives before. The other department leader didn't say anything. Without really thinking through my next statement, I put out there, "So, all ten of these initiatives are what we as an overall organization need to, should, ought to, and must do. What happens if we don't?"

He said, "Well, I guess we'll just continue them next year. Or change them up. Or go on to something else."

There was no point in continuing to ask questions in this situation. The tension was thick. But my mind was roiling. "Need, should, ought, and must." I use these verbs all the time, and I actually don't really mean anything by them. I'm pulling rank. Establishing my territory. Setting a standard. I do it to my children and wife. I do it to my organization workers. I do it in my department's activities.

I decided to attempt not to use "need, should, ought, or must" unless no other concept was possible.

I would choose what I **might** do. What is possible for me?

What I **can** do. What am I capable to do?

What I **will** do. What am I willing to do?

Might, can, and **will** replaced **need, should, ought,** and **must** in my working vocabulary. It changed my thinking. It changed how I lived.

These changes in how you word your thoughts are very hard to make, because the use of verbs of intended obligation saturate our conventional awareness.

Let's revisit the first three Storylines from the Introduction, in light of the whole concept.

Storyline 1*: You are out for an evening walk, and see several neighbors in a tight circle, obviously having a conversation about something. It seems at a glance that it's pretty serious. You walk up and greet them in a friendly manner, but no one says anything back immediately. That's strange. One lady dabs a tear from her eyes. After a few strained seconds, one guy tells you that your neighbor two doors down from your house has committed suicide at his home, today, right around noon. You are stunned. Shocked! You just talked to him last weekend and he seemed "fine." He appeared to you to have everything a modern person could ever dream of having. But he took his own life. The klatch of folks begins speculating on his depression, his problems, his history...None of these speculations adds up at all in your mind. Why do people do that? Not only why do people who seem to have it all together commit suicide, but why does everyone seem to believe it's OK to chatter and gossip about why they think it happened? Seriously, why do people do that?

The questions raised by everyone near and far connected to a person who commits suicide are intense, important, and often unanswerable. When a person attempts suicide and survives, some of the same issues can be raised, but the answers from the person, the family, the professionals, and the observers may be inadequate or inaccurate.

Even when a person committing suicide leaves a note, or had communicated his or her thoughts, feelings, and intentions, the question many family and friends still are haunted by is, "Why? Why did that person do that?"

That question cannot be answered sufficiently in a book like this. Each individual person has a distinct set of capacities within all ten of their senses of perception, their five emotional systems, their motivations and behaviors they are capable of, and willing to, do. Sometimes, a hasty, ill-formed plan of action, designed to call attention to an overwhelming circumstance, has permanent consequences: a person in trouble cries out but dies as a result of the cry. Sometimes, the plan for a personal death is logical (at least to the person considering it) and is carried out with precision.

A suicide event can be designed by the person committing it to inflict a maximum amount of pain, fear, hatred, or other harmful outcomes on the family or friends who are left behind to struggle with the self-inflicted death. Sometimes, a suicide is designed to appear purely accidental, or in such a way as to lessen all of the traumatic issues that can result.

Let's look at just five theoretical reasons why a person might attempt or commit suicide, based on the Complex of Emotional Systems. Please keep in the forefront of your thinking that these emotions are described from the viewpoint of the person struggling with issues and not from any outsider's viewpoint.

1. Acceptance: The person reviews his or her life and concludes everything that can be done has been done. Life is complete, and the person has accepted such an idea as true. Ending one's life on one's own terms is an appropriate end to a satisfying lifespan.

2. Exposure: The person is facing some source of legal, social, or personal terror that is extremely more severe, in his or her mind, than the mysterious safety of death. Not wanting the process of dying to add to the fears at hand, a self-inflicted death seems to lessen the risks.

3. Empowerment: The person is completely filled with self-hatred or a rage toward others that is excessive and destructive. The person might act to wreak destruction and havoc on others first and himself or herself as an outcome or commit suicide first and do so in a way that results in tremendous pain in others' lives.

4. Depletion: Commonly, suicide is framed as an outcome of depression, a mental or biochemical state of mind. However, the person may have eroded his or her personal resources in one or more areas, neglecting any kind of healthy replenishment and restoration processes, resulting in a collapsing sense of the self and the world. The person may believe he or she has nothing left with which to fight, to push, to try.

5. Celebration: The person is a thrill-seeker of the highest order, living day-to-day on the edge of exciting and dangerous activities that continually stimulate euphoria and an adrenaline rush. Death may be seen as the final frontier to experience, and the person's personal belief system includes continued thrills on the other side of death. So a suicide merely allows for continuous euphoria.

Which of these explanations is correct? You don't really know. As human beings, most people want a sense of closure, an adequate explanation that allows our minds and hearts a sense of peace that the world makes sense. It's not always possible to achieve that outcome.

You want to figure out why your neighbor, who seemed "fine" a few days ago, committed suicide. Could you have prevented it? Seen some warning signs? Been a little friendlier to give your neighbor a bit of hope? Is it your fault? That becomes a vital question many of those left behind by a suicide of a relative or friend wonder.

One stark aspect of every suicide situation is absolutely true: no one, even the victim, knows all of the variables and factors that are in play in the circumstances of a person's life. Suicide is a permanent solution to a temporary situation, as perceived by the person committing it. Its roots and its fruits, the causes and the outcomes, are extremely complicated and take immense effort to detangle the interwoven factors and issues.

Much more remains to be covered on this important matter.

Storyline 2: You are out to lunch with a couple of friends. While you three are in a secluded booth, one of your friends begins to cry quietly. You ask, "What's wrong?" After an interminable thirty seconds of silence among the three of you, during which you hardly want to breathe, your friend mumbles, "I've been having an affair with someone at work. I think I'm going to lose my marriage." The other friend, stony-faced with no apparent emotion at all, says, "Aw, don't worry about that. I'm having an affair too. It's no big deal." Then both friends look at you, like you're supposed to say something now. Why do people act that way?

In the moment, you have a few clues to work with. The first friend is crying, showing potent emotion. The key emotion your friend declared is fear: *"I think I'm going to lose my marriage."* Do not make assumptions for your friend, although that is very easy to do. Allow the friend to have the privilege of declaring his or her own situation.

You can listen. Ask questions, as might seem appropriate. Get answers. You can even simply reflect whatever your friend says, using the same words your friend chooses. Ask better questions. You do not need to come up with the answers.

"I don't know," is an acceptable listening response. "I don't care," is not. *You: "You're having an affair? You think you might lose your marriage over this?"*

Your friend responds, "This is killing me."

You: "This sounds really painful for you. What bothers you the most?"

Your conversation is starting out in the area of Depletion, since the word chosen by your friend is "lose." Your friend also added "killing," so you can explore other words within Empowerment.

But your primary role is to listen creatively, with engagement to the moment, giving support within the realm of the emotional system your friend has expressed. Depletion is about healing, recovery, or restoration. Empowerment is about change or power. You can listen without suggesting outcomes or providing advice.

Your other friend may provide some kind of counterpoint, or interference. Let that friend stand on their own position, without you trying to explain or criticize.

Storyline 3: In your work group, one individual is quite skilled, obviously intelligent, has a great work ethic and very positive productivity. But that person finds ways of "joking" about co-workers, bosses, vendors, customers, passers-by, politicians, family members, and the cleaning staff. Pretty much anybody. But the "jokes" come out in ways that are insulting, crude, mean-spirited, and totally unnecessary. These are always made in under-the-breath comments that are intended only for you to hear and laugh at. The jokes are actually funny occasionally and show intuitive insight. The comments never actually cross the line into reportable violations of company policy.

They are never heard by others for verification of your potential reporting.
This person seems to undermine relationships with just about everybody,
but not openly...So, you know the feigned compliments and encouragements
that occasionally come from the offender toward others are part of the great
joking mind-set. There's nothing you can say or do about it. Why do people
act that way?

This co-worker uses attempts at humor of the kind that is amused by others' pain, injury, misfortune, or discomfort. The use of comments like this are a power play, by someone who struggles with a deflated self-value. Using secrecy and collusion with you, by side comments or private jokes, you also are being set up in a power play. Instead of dealing with an emotional system of Celebration, where humor and comedy belong, you are dealing with a barrage of Empowerment emotions. Recognize that the issues surround the focal point of power and control.

If you do nothing except passively accept the comments without repeating them or aligning yourself with that viewpoint, you might think you are avoiding the power play. You are not. You're falling into it. Nonresistance is seen as compliance, even agreement, by power players. You can be direct. *"Stop the comments now. I do not want to hear one more joke or insult from you about anyone."*

If that doesn't work (which it probably won't), you can increase the force of your comment. *"You are not willing to stop making those jokes and comments. I am writing down and dating every comment you make. I want the record and the verification recorded. You will stop making those comments to me from this point forward. Do not make them again."*

Keep your record privately and in a safe location. If that doesn't work (which it might, or that person may simply pick another target listener), be sure your list is up-to-date, and report your record within the appropriate systems.

This kind of situation is tough. When you understand the primary realm in which you are engaged, you can be successful at working toward the outcomes of that realm.

Wrap-Up

This book is about the human experience. It focuses on one key aspect of how human beings experience life: emotions. It presents a sequence by which people develop their experience of life:

1. The Complex of Perceptions

2. The Complex of Emotional Systems

3. The Complex of Motivations

4. The Complex of Behaviors

While these four complexes initially engage in this sequence, they become interactive, each complex affecting all the other complexes in dynamic ways.

The main focus of this book is on the Five Basic Emotional Systems:

1. Acceptance – "Love" and Its Family

2. Exposure – "Fear" and Its Friends

3. Empowerment – "Anger" and Its Teammates

4. Depletion – "Sadness" and Its Co-Workers

5. Celebration – "Happiness" and Its Neighbors

A number of tools have been scattered through this book that you can use in your personal and professional life;

1. Set the Best Goal

2. Emotional Neutrality

3. The Ladder Principle

4. The Question Sequence

5. The Vocabulary Choice

All of these concepts and tools have been presented in this book in their simplest forms. Go to www.WDPATW.com to find additional in-depth materials. You can also request Dr. Myke Merrill for live training in your organization, or for individual consultation. The application of the concepts and principles will be tailored to your specific situation.

If you have questions that have come to you about this book or its concepts, please send an email with your questions to:

ask@wdpatw.com

For scheduling Dr. Myke Merrill as a speaker, send an email of inquiry, with as many specifics as you can include, to inquiries@drmyke.com. I look forward to hearing from you.

Bulk sales of this book are possible at a reduced price. Please send an inquiry about bulk sales to inquiries@drmyke.com for additional details.

If you read and enjoyed this book, please consider writing a review for Amazon.com. Your insights and reviews are greatly appreciated.

Dr. Myke Merrill originally wanted to have a professional career in some field based on math for two reasons: 1) every problem has a right answer, and 2) if a person's brain is good at math, finding that answer is easy. (All you doctors of theoretical math, please do not write and excoriate this overly simplified analysis here. This is an adolescent thinking process.) When he got to college at Rochester Institute of Technology, he found those two aspects incredibly boring. (Again, don't ravage these immature opinions.) So he decided to work with people, initially as a clinical psychologist. This inclination was based on two opposite points to those above: 1) there is no "right answer" when it comes to people and what they are dealing with or how they deal with it, and 2) no matter how good a person's brain is at people skills, working with people is never easy.

Myke transferred to a smaller college to be trained as a pastor, graduating *magna cum laude* with a Bachelor of Arts in Religion and Philosophy, and a minor in psychology. He graduated with a Master's of Divinity degree from Asbury Theological Seminary, with academic honors. After two years as an associate, he and his growing family located in Hilton, NY, and are still based there. He earned a Doctor of Ministry degree from Northeastern Seminary with his dissertation, *"The Five Basic Emotions: A New Systems Approach."*

Seizing on a wide variety of opportunities, he taught as an adjunct instructor in a local college for 29 years, directed regional and national youth programs for 20 years, owned a restaurant for seven years, a sign company for 18 years, and wrote 22 books and training manuals. He has traveled extensively to train others across the United States and in ten other countries. He co-owns a school system in Honduras. He still rides a 1965 Schwinn Continental bicycle with about 60,000 miles on it so far, which he bought as a twelve-year old. He plays a nice 12-string Martin guitar.

He loves playing softball. He hates asparagus.

He's pretty much just like you.

Made in the USA
Lexington, KY
14 December 2019

58566221R00083